D1539795

Praise for Seeking the Calm in the Storm

"Judy Bardwick is a teacher of the first order. Like all effective teachers, she gives us perspective on the world we face and instills the belief that we can bring order out of the chaos surrounding our lives. Most important, she shows that we are not alone in our struggle. We're all overwhelmed with the demands of this noisy, nonstop world—but we need not be imprisoned by it."

—JIM COLLINS
Author of Good to Great, *coauthor* Built to Last

"Judy Bardwick has captured the essence of the challenges of our fast-paced, 24/7 lives and clearly articulated how people and organizations can respond effectively. Her assessment of the challenges we face resonates; her proposals for our future enrich, enable, and help us find some calm amidst our daily storms.

"She understands the pressures of the world around us, the liabilities of modern society. But even more, she points us in a direction to help organizations and individuals change. She reminds and encourages us to take control of our destiny. The work is realistic, clever, insightful, and will be useful to us every day."

—DAVID ULRICH
Author of The HR Scorecard *and named* BusinessWeek's
#1 Business Guru in the world

"Judith Bardwick's book is a rich and informed foray into the wildly turbulent, 24/7 world facing every individual and organization. It is a splendid read because of its thick wisdom. Beyond that, it's a comforting read because it makes one feel less alone and that it's possible to understand, and to some degree master, the context of this swirling and volatile world."

—WARREN BENNIS
University Professor, USC and coauthor of
Geeks and Geezers

SEEKING THE CALM IN THE STORM

ISBN 0-13-009031-X

FINANCIAL TIMES
Prentice Hall

In an increasingly competitive world, it is quality
of thinking that gives an edge—an idea that opens new
doors, a technique that solves a problem, or an insight
that simply helps make sense of it all.

We work with leading authors in the various arenas
of business and finance to bring cutting-edge thinking
and best learning practice to a global market.

It is our goal to create world-class print publications
and electronic products that give readers
knowledge and understanding which can then be
applied, whether studying or at work.

To find out more about our business
products, you can visit us at www.ft-ph.com

Pearson
Education

SEEKING THE CALM IN THE STORM

Managing Chaos in Your Business Life

DR . JUDITH M. BARDWICK, PHD

FINANCIAL TIMES
Prentice Hall

An Imprint of PEARSON EDUCATION
London • New York • San Francisco • Toronto • Sydney
Tokyo • Singapore • Hong Kong • Cape Town • Madrid •
Paris • Milan • Munich • Amsterdam
www.ft-ph.com

Library of Congress Cataloging-in-Publication Data

Bardwick, Judith M.,
    Seeking the calm in the storm: managing chaos in your business life / Judith M. Bardwick.
        p. cm.
    Includes bibliographical references and index.
    ISBN: 0-13-009031-X
        1. Information Technology--Social aspects. 2. Management. I. Title.

    T58.5 .B365 2002
    650.1--dc21   2002022741

Editorial/Production Supervision: *Jan H. Schwartz*
VP, Executive Editor: *Tim Moore*
Executive Marketing Manager: *Bryan Gambrel*
Manufacturing Manager: *Alexis R. Heydt-Long*
Buyer: *Maura Zaldivar*
Cover Design Director: *Jerry Votta*
Cover Design: *Nina Scuderi*
Editorial Assistant: *Allyson Kloss*

©2002 by Financial Times Prentice Hall
An imprint of Pearson Education, Inc.
Upper Saddle River, NJ 07458

Financial Times Prentice Hall books are widely used by corporations and government agencies for training, marketing, and resale.

The publisher offers discounts on this book when ordered in bulk quantities.
For more information, contact: Corporate Sales Department, Phone: 800-382-3419;
Fax: 201-236-7141; Email: corpsales@prenhall.com; or write: Prentice Hall PTR,
Corp. Sales Dept., One Lake Street, Upper Saddle River, NJ 07458.

Printed in the United States of America

10 9 8 7 6 5 4 3 2 1

ISBN 0-13-009031-X

Pearson Education LTD.
Pearson Education Australia PTY, Limited
Pearson Education Singapore, Pte. Ltd.
Pearson Education North Asia Ltd.
Pearson Education Canada, Ltd.
Pearson Educación de Mexico, S.A. de C.V.
Pearson Education—Japan
Pearson Education Malaysia, Pte. Ltd.

FINANCIAL TIMES PRENTICE HALL BOOKS

For more information, please go to www.ft-ph.com

Dr. Judith M. Bardwick, PhD
Seeking the Calm in the Storm: Managing Chaos in Your Business Life

Thomas L. Barton, William G. Shenkir, and Paul L. Walker
*Making Enterprise Risk Management Pay Off:
How Leading Companies Implement Risk Management*

Deirdre Breakenridge
Cyberbranding: Brand Building in the Digital Economy

William C. Byham, Audrey B. Smith, and Matthew J. Paese
*Grow Your Own Leaders: How to Identify, Develop, and Retain
Leadership Talent*

Jonathan Cagan and Craig M. Vogel
*Creating Breakthrough Products: Innovation from Product Planning
to Program Approval*

Subir Chowdhury
The Talent Era: Achieving a High Return on Talent

Sherry Cooper
Ride the Wave: Taking Control in a Turbulent Financial Age

James W. Cortada
*21st Century Business: Managing and Working
in the New Digital Economy*

James W. Cortada
*Making the Information Society: Experience, Consequences,
and Possibilities*

Aswath Damodaran
*The Dark Side of Valuation: Valuing Old Tech, New Tech,
and New Economy Companies*

Henry A. Davis and William W. Sihler
Financial Turnarounds: Preserving Enterprise Value

Sarv Devaraj and Rajiv Kohli
*The IT Payoff: Measuring the Business Value
of Information Technology Investments*

Jaime Ellertson and Charles W. Ogilvie
*Frontiers of Financial Services: Turning Customer Interactions
Into Profits*

W. Alan Randolph and Barry Z. Posner
  Checkered Flag Projects: 10 Rules for Creating and Managing Projects that Win, Second Edition

Stephen P. Robbins
  The Truth About Managing People…And Nothing but the Truth

Eric G. Stephan and Wayne R. Pace
  Powerful Leadership: How to Unleash the Potential in Others and Simplify Your Own Life

Jonathan Wight
  Saving Adam Smith: A Tale of Wealth, Transformation, and Virtue

Yoram J. Wind and Vijay Mahajan, with Robert Gunther
  Convergence Marketing: Strategies for Reaching the New Hybrid Consumer

This book is dedicated with love to
Rachel Elizabeth Ahearn
and
Grace Elizabeth Bardwick

The next, next generation!

CONTENTS

FOREWORD

America has two generations for whom Pearl Harbor has no emotional power and almost as little cognitive clout. It is not surprising that the nation developed an assumption of invulnerability. The terrorist attacks of September 11, 2001 changed that: Where buildings had pierced the sky, now there was only rubble. Where 50,000 people had worked, there was only impenetrable dust: Dust to dust... but there was no solace in that. Our sophisticated and powerful society had not protected its people. In our primitive, fundamental, and atavistic core, we were assaulted. Whether in New York or California, Europe, Asia, or Australia, our sense of reality, our notions of how things are supposed to happen, were besieged.

I wanted to visit Ground Zero, to see it for myself, because this was a transformational event, one that would forever change how people saw and structured reality. I'd had that experience once before, on December 7, 1941, when I was a little girl. Though it was forever ago, I will always remember that night. My parents were hunched close to the radio, faces somber and disbelieving, saying again and again to no one, "This is war... this is war." September 11, 2001: "This is war."

On September 27, just 16 days after the World Trade Center towers fell and the people within them were lost, my friend Anita Ross and I set out to get as close to Ground Zero as we could.

Like most everyone else, we had spent days glued to the television, our minds not grasping the images that played on the screen. We had watched the same scenes over and over and over, as though repetition could make sense of the incomprehensible; as though repetition could dull the agony everyone felt but could not express. This pain was beyond words; language doesn't have words to describe what is unimaginable.

By September 27, New Yorkers as well as the rest of the country had begun to roll up their sleeves and go back to work. Men and women wore red, white, and blue ribbons on their lapels. The city wasn't normal but it was getting there. There were people on the streets and in the stores and sub-ways—just not as many. People were walking, but their strides weren't as purposeful. Even on the subway, people were friendly and helpful. In the face of the assault, helpful-ness, friendliness, and patriotism were rising just as they did a little more than half a century ago.

We took the subway as far as we could and around 4:30 in the afternoon, got out to walk the mile or so to where the towers had stood. We walked deliberately, one foot slowly following the other. We gradually became aware of a faint odor that became progressively stronger. It was the smell of smoke, of things burned. Everywhere we looked we saw whitish-gray powder, the ashes of paper, wood, and insulation.

Men and women in police uniforms and military garb kept telling us to keep moving, not to stop, not to take pictures. But people continued to move as slowly as possible, lingering and staring as long as they could. As we got closer, where a block ended and was cut by a cross street, we looked to the right and there it was. It was exactly what we had seen on television, and yet it wasn't. The size of it, oh, the size of it! Enormous steel girders were twisted—wrapped into coils like an unruly Slinky. The two remaining pieces of the façade remained incongruously, incredulously, upright. We lingered as long as we could. We couldn't believe it...but we couldn't leave.

There was everything to see and nothing to be seen. Ambulances weren't rolling and people weren't running. There were no sirens, there was no clash of grinding gears. In the slow-moving crowd of observers, there were no cries of anguish, no tears, and no shouts of retribution. We heard soft voices in many languages, but more than anything there was the solemnity of silence. This assault was too big to lend itself to words.

We had gone as close as we could and had seen as much as possible. It was time to leave and yet, it was not time to go. Why couldn't we leave when there was nothing more to see? Part of it was the need for repetition, to see the same thing over and over and make it real. By making it real, we stripped it of the unbelievable. As the destruction became real—but finite—it ceased being the untamable awfulness of nightmares.

There was also another reason for staying. The enormity of this tragedy and outrage are not communicated well by ideas, words, or even pictures. It was only in its presence, that we could feel what happened. In the face of it, it became impossible to diminish the importance of what we had experienced. We couldn't trivialize what we had seen by giving it short shrift, so we dignified the experience by staying with it.

There was silence there and slowness and finally, dignity because the place where the towers stood was already a shrine. Religious or not, we bowed our heads. What will soothe here will be ritual: Scottish bagpipes, Amazing Grace, flags at half mast, and a perpetual flame.

The assault did not weaken America. Instead, the narcissism, materialism, arrogance, and pettiness that became too characteristic of the United States is giving way to purposefulness, unity, and resolve. The assault on material America has awakened a keen sense of our history and the very meaning of the nation. Death has generated community. At least that's true for now.

The 21st century is a world of permanent turbulence. The world's economies, like its geopolitics, like terrorism, are borderless. Jets, phones, faxes, computers, and pagers have made any event, anywhere, our event. Everywhere, in everything, there are accelerating changes in alliances, markets, technologies, competition, and opportunities. Our sensibilities about what to expect in business, as in the world, are continuously challenged.

With unrelenting change and unpredictability, it is hard to feel confident that we know and understand what is happening, it becomes hard to make decisions and act on them, and it becomes hard to sustain a basic sense of well-being.

Yet the world of permanent turbulence is our world: We have to live in it, we have to work in it, and we have to flourish within it. The goal of the first half of this book is to achieve greater clarity about a world, especially the world of business, that is in a permanent state of transformation. When we perceive these realities clearly, we've taken the first step to regaining a sense of control over what's happening. In the last half of the book we'll begin to formulate recommendations about what we must do as a nation, as organizations, and as individuals in order for us to succeed under the stressful conditions of unending, swift, and major change.

Acknowledgments

Although authors initiate the writing of a book, it takes a team to finish it. I'm especially grateful to the following people:

Allen Armstrong, Captain, USCG Ret., my husband, for his irreplaceable support.

Peter Bardwick, my son, and my brother, Stephen Hardis, for their essays and interest.

Tim Moore, my publisher, for his incisive insight.

Henning Gutmann, my agent, for his wisdom and guidance.

Russ Hall, my editor, for his transformation of the manuscript.

Corinne Gregory, my technical reviewer, for her grasp of what I was trying to say.

Helen Bloomfield, my assistant, for accomplishments that are always above and beyond.

Jan Schwartz, Production Editor, for pulling it all together and mastering every detail while under unremitting time pressure.

I'd also like to thank *BusinessWeek* for permission to reprint their illuminating article "Like It Or Not, You've Got Mail"; *Forbes ASAP* for permission to reprint a snippet of Eric Pfeiffer's ode, " 'Tis a Joy to Be Simple..."; *Fortune* for permission to reprint an excerpt from John Reed's excellent article, "Reflections on a Culture Clash"; HarperCollins publishers for permission to reprint an excerpt from Barbara Kingsolver's award-winning novel, *The Poisonwood Bible*; New York Magazine for permission to reprint part of Michael Wolf's insightful essay on "the e-decade"; and Random House/Bantam Books publishers for permission to reprint from Elizabeth George's excellent book *In Pursuit of the Proper Sinner*.

For these authors' thoughtful work I am most grateful.

INTRODUCTION

In the wake of the September 11, 2001, assault on America's sense of security, many organizations found that even though they had not lost anyone to the terrorist's attacks, their employees were calling out for emotional help.[1] It's perfectly normal and reasonable that many people felt vulnerable and anxious in response to that harrowing and senseless chaos. But I think that the crisis assault on many people's sense of well-being was actually the last straw, one added to chronic anxiety generated by the uncertainty and rising demands of a borderless economy.

The most important goal for most Americans—and most people everywhere—is to achieve economic and other forms of security for their families and themselves. It is very stressful to work longer and harder, make decisions faster and faster, and never know for sure if it's enough to make you safe and to keep you secure. I think it was a relief to many people when their sense of unease, anxiety, depression, and exhaustion became a national mood and they could finally ask for help. Too many people are feeling chronically stressed.

We're stressed because we've lost the sanctuary of privacy. Personally, even though I don't carry a laptop or a pager when I'm on the road, the bright red message light on my hotel phone blinks stridently. If I forget to turn it off, my cell phone rings at 30,000 feet. It takes several hours a day to get through email. I'm awakened at absurd hours, in remote places, on weekends and vacations, because distance doesn't matter anymore and everyone is available to anyone at anytime, day or night.

My world has changed permanently because the world changes instantaneously.

In the relatively recent past, in the decades following World War II, the economy of the United States flourished, as did most of our large corporations. America dominated the world's economy and with few international competitors, there was no sense of urgency about doing things better, faster, or differently. In comparison with the present, conditions were comfortable, organizations were frequently complacent, change—if any—was slow and gradual, and a five-year plan had some credibility. In those stable conditions, people felt they had a reasonable amount of control in their life and they understood what was happening because it wasn't much different from what they had seen before. From the early 1950s to the early 1990s, these conditions were widespread in America and much of the rest of the world.

Some people and some organizations continue to behave as if nothing has changed: There's still no sense of urgency, time is not money, there are endless amounts of both, and creating a report that leads to nothing is still considered "work."

When I moved to San Diego in 1981 I learned that building a new airport was such a controversial issue that nothing had been decided and nothing had been built for almost 40 years. Our airport, Lindbergh Field, is currently the smallest airport of any major American city. It has only one runway, which is glaringly inadequate for America's sixth largest city, and that's especially true in the winter when the city is susceptible to fog. In the past five years, our previous mayor, Susan Golding, led the effort to pour more than $400 million into refurbishing an airport with one runway that has no room to expand.

I thought that was about as bad as it could get, but I was wrong. On November 28, 2001, *The San Diego Union-Tribune* printed a small article that it buried in Section 2.[2] The Port Commission of San Diego authorized funds for a $1.9 million analysis of the future of our airport. That report will be added to the more than two dozen studies involving Lindbergh Field that have been completed since 1943. Those studies have led to neither decisions nor actions. The issue of San Diego's airport has not been resolved for almost 60 years.

In general, governments—like colleges and universities, most of the public school system, or the regulated part of utilities—remain bastions of stable conditions. But, for the majority of people, stable, predictable, controllable conditions are going or are gone.

Beginning in the early 1980s, the business equivalent of the earth's tectonic plates started shifting. Extraordinary advances in technology, especially the advent of the user-friendly World Wide Web in the early 1990s, created a borderless economy in which time and distance no longer create protection from competition and change.

Borderlessness is the opposite of stability: It creates conditions of accelerating change and thus of unpredictability. It is the borderlessness of the world that has created permanent turbulence. Increasing numbers of organizations and people everywhere face ever-increasing competition and accelerating core change.

The borderless world is fundamentally one of unprecedented opportunity—and of uncertainty, turbulence, and a lack of personal and organizational control. The sheer amount, speed, and magnitude of basic change is unprecedented. Ten years ago no one would have predicted major layoffs in the midst of great times, or three-year-olds with their own computers, or cell phones with a personal telephone number that you carried everywhere. Now we take these changes, and change itself, for granted. But, today's reality is increasingly disruptive and immensely demanding, and that generates stress and uncertainty for an awful lot of people.[3]

Although people and organizations in stable times think they're dealing with major changes, the pace is slow; change is gradual, not transformational; there's plenty of time to do things thoroughly, to analyze and plan, and to act with thoughtful premeditation. In stable times, if nothing much actually happens that's too bad, but still okay because competitors aren't trying to eat you for lunch. Because organizations and their members feel the world is a pretty predictable place, they also believe that it makes sense to create long-term plans, 5- and 10-year strategic analyses, for example. Perhaps most important of all, gradual, incremental change does not involve any major disruptions from what is already familiar, it doesn't invalidate what people already know, and it doesn't generate fear and anxiety.

Borderless conditions—continuously accelerating basic change, unpredictability, uncertainty, and risk—are both exciting and scary. They're exhilarating for confident people who thrive on risk and find stability boring. People who are already confident and resilient may well flourish during fast cycles of economic growth and destruction. But for people who had long enjoyed and still long for the calm of stable conditions, the transformation of the "Prudential Rock"[4] to quicksand is very frightening.

In addition to technological changes, the 1980s and 1990s saw a huge growth in international trading treaties, improvements in transportation and containerization, privatization, and deregulation. As a result, work now migrates anywhere it can be done well and at an appropriate cost. The help desk you call is very likely to be located in India, Ireland, or Jamaica, and you never know that. There are fewer hurdles to setting up shop down the block or around the world. There are endless pressures to quickly get costs down and ever-rising requirements to do things faster and better. Competition increases faster than does opportunity.

Borderless conditions expand opportunities while they simultaneously unleash fiercely competitive forces. Increasingly, ideas and money move in a nanosecond, surging toward areas in which potentials are high and fleeing from commitments where profit is negligible. The result is *churn*, high rates of job and industry growth and destruction. That's why huge layoffs continued during the great bull market and soaring economic years of the 1980s and 1990s. Within the same corporation, for example, divisions were started and other divisions were closed because they no longer had a future.

Most of all, reality becomes increasingly Darwinian. A borderless economy is far more results-driven than the no-consequence business culture that's typical in stable conditions.[5] When money speeds to arenas where the profit potential is high and flees from where there is no potential, the result is instability. Huge layoffs, plant closings, restructuring, and outsourcing replace job security and tenure. Web speed becomes normal, and change, turbulence, and unpredictability all accelerate. That's a high-risk reality.

Ironically, capitalism's essential harshness produces its very vitality. In the new reality, sine wavelike cycles of both creation and destruction are occurring swiftly.

The economist Joseph Schumpeter observed that capitalism is in a constant state of flux in which entrepreneurs introduce changes that force incumbents to adapt or die.[6] Capitalism continuously destroys whatever already exists and replaces it with something new and better.[7]

Stress and Anxiety Are Rising

Although America's willingness to change, to embrace rather than resist a borderless reality was responsible for the nation's economic ascendance in the 1990s, it was not without cost. Even in the second half of the 1990s, when job growth was so large that the unemployment rate was below four percent, layoffs were still as large as they had been in the slowdown of 1991 and 1992.[8] In a borderless global economy, hard-earned knowledge and skills are often swiftly outdated. There is relentless pressure on individuals to do more and learn more and be cutting edge. The pace of work keeps accelerating.

In November 2001, XEROX ran full page ads in business magazines that exalted multitasking: "If you could print while you scan, copy while you email, scan while you fax, and do it all while printing up to 3x faster...you'd be smiling too."[9] Real downtime is disappearing because work pervades many people's home life.

The fundamental conditions of today's economy are inherently demanding. Product cycles are short and competitive advantages are fleeting. Most organizations face relentless pressure to create major innovations that will give them a competitive advantage if only for a short time. When normalcy is the sense that the world is unpredictable, inexplicable, and uncontrollable, many people are too stressed and anxiety-ridden to work or live well.

Nonetheless, I am optimistic about the foundations of the American economy and in the resilience of its people. Despite the wave of dot-com closings I believe there is an improved, new economy in the United States and other nations.[10] It is knowledge-based and inflation-resistant because of technological improvements in productivity. Deregulation and privatization encourage entrepreneurs to think large and create the next "big thing." The future improves on the past, but the path is never a straight line.

But, a borderless Darwinian economy is so stressful that most people need some grounding, somewhere in their world, so they have some sense of control and confidence. It is my task in this book to examine the new economic world we've created in order to figure out what will enable people to flourish in their private lives as well as their economically productive roles. Somehow, work and life have to be joined as human goals.

ENDNOTES

1. Martinez, Barbara, Winslow, Ron, and Peterson, Andrea, "Far From Site, Employees Seek Emotional Help," *The Wall Street Journal*, October 5, 2001, pp. B1, B3.

2. Powell, Ronald W., "Port Commission Earmarks Funds for Latest Airport Study," *The San Diego Union-Tribune*, November 28, 2001, p. B2.

3. The military diminish people's sense of having little or no control by training in conditions of little visibility in which the unexpected is ordinary and everyone in the field adapts and initiates where they stand.

4. The Prudential Insurance Company likens itself to the Rock of Gibraltar.

5. For a full discussion of the no-consequence culture that characterizes organizations in stable conditions or those that are monopolies like government, see my book *Danger in the Comfort Zone*, AMACOM, NY, 1991. The paperback edition was published in 1995.

6. Useem, Jerry, "Dead Thinkers' Society," *Business 2.0*, November 2001, pp. 132–134.

7. Federal Reserve Chairman Alan Greenspan has described as remarkable the 1980s and 1990s acceleration of this process of creative destruction in which capital is shifted away from failing or outmoded technologies into those that are cutting edge.

8. Morris, Betsy, "White Collar Bues," *Fortune*, July 23, 2001, pp. 98–110.

9. *Business 2.0*, November 2001, p. 151.

10. Coy, Peter, "The New Economy: How Real Is It?," *BusinessWeek*, August 27, 2001, pp. 80–85.

1

WHERE'S MY PERSONAL TIME AND SPACE?

- COMPARTMENTALIZING STRENGTHENS BOUNDARIES
- BEING ACCESSIBLE DIS- SOLVES THEM
- SHOULD WORK AND PRIVATE SPHERES BE BOUND OR FLUID?

I can work anywhere, anytime, day or night. I'm in control. I'm always accessible. I'm never off duty. I'm not in control.

Some people enjoy fluid lines between work and their personal lives because they find it interesting, lively, and efficient. They try to achieve balance in their lives by dissolving boundaries among their commitments because they think that lets them use their time better and get more done in both spheres. Although that means they're always accessible, they feel in control because they're always in contact.

1

Other people gain control because they're really good at compartmentalization; they shore up boundaries. I learned to compartmentalize when I was a graduate student and had infants. I'd go to work as soon as the baby fell asleep and stop immediately when the baby woke up. Because I had no time to waste, I became very productive. But it was necessary for me to make a hard distinction between work and personal time because when I was at work, I was totally focused on work, but when it was my time, I didn't think about work at all. I needed that separation because only in my personal time could I thoroughly relax and savor some desperately needed downtime.

I'm not as wired as some of the people I know. We have four computers (one being a laptop), cable for Internet access, a fax machine, and a cell phone. But I don't have a pager and I don't usually carry the phone or the laptop. I don't want to be accessible to everyone, everywhere, anytime. Lately that makes me eccentric since about 123 million Americans are married to their mobile phones because, unlike me, they do want to be reachable by anyone, all the time.[1] Technology makes it easy for people to work in their cars, on boats, or on planes. You can work as easily at your desk at home as in your office. If you carry a pager, cell phone, or laptop, it doesn't matter where you are.

Sitting in an airplane, I have often watched as most of the people around me stare at the screens of their laptops, fingers flying, pausing only briefly to either study what's on the screen or reach ahead for the phone on the back of the seat in front of them to call someone, somewhere on earth. Once, my seatmate, a lawyer who never stopped working observed, "I know we work harder and longer but I'm not at all sure we work better. There's no time just to think."

For increasing numbers of people, the traditional boundary between work time and place and personal time and space is gone. Although this flexibility can increase productivity and one's sense of control, it can also decrease any feelings of control and lead to burnout.

Beginning around 1992 or 1993, professionals and some members of management started carrying cell phones, pagers, and laptops. By the middle of the decade the Web made the Internet easy to use and Web sites proliferated. The amount of information and communications that entered our computers exploded. Choices—What to buy? Where to buy it? Where to go? How to arrange it?—multiplied geometrically. With information easily available and secretaries and assistants gone, we became suddenly responsible for knowing about things, making choices, and creating arrangements that someone else had always done. At home many people did the same thing and dispensed with travel agents' services.

In stable times, we were occasionally overloaded. Now many people are overloaded all of the time. We have data overload, emotional overload, sensory overload, and responsibility overload.

The "anywhere-ness" of most people's jobs is a source of both flexibility and overload. Personal and work: Should the spheres be boundaried or fluid? People need to know whether they flourish or implode with continuous input, emails, and interruptions because that's a choice people need to—and should—make.

WORK ANYWHERE

In the 1990s, the development of tools like the laptop computer, the cell phone, and high-speed modems resulted in extraordinary workplace flexibility. Laptops gave people immediate access to their organization's intranet, their email, and the Internet. With the proliferation of the Web, people could send and receive reports, analyses, voice mail, and email, whenever and wherever they wanted to. Technology became very sophisticated.

Telecommuting—working electronically outside of the office—is increasingly common. In 2001, 28.8 million people described themselves as telecommuters.[2] A recent survey of 1,000 Internet users found that 82 percent of those who participated said they had a home office, 69 percent reported they worked in their home office at least once a day, and 43 percent observed that they were spending more time in that home office than they had a year ago.[3] The U.S. Census Bureau reported that about 17 million small businesses were home-based in 2001.[4] More and more, work is moving to the worker instead of the worker moving to the work.

Not commuting (especially during rush hour), setting your own schedule, being able to cope with household emergencies...*having more flexibility and control over your time*, can be telecommuting's most valuable outcome.

Having more control over the conditions of work, including when and where they work, is a major gain, especially to caregivers. For many people—two-paycheck families, single parents, and children of aging parents, for example—gaining more control over their time in order to meet demanding and important life as well as work responsibilities can outweigh other priorities. That is family friendly and a boon to everyone.

There are also negative aspects to alternative work arrangements or simply working at home. First, it makes you interruptible. That's not just because you're physically there, although that's important. Working at home communicates something unprofessional, an activity that's not to be taken as seriously as something that's done in an office. Being casually dressed contributes to that perception. As a result, people often feel free to interrupt. I keep telling people, unsuccessfully, that when I'm in my writing office—the one without a phone jack—I am out of town.

Anyone who works at home usually works long hours and on weekends. That's partly for pragmatic reasons: Today, work is never finished and it's hard to ignore when you have an office in your house. There are also psychological reasons why telecommuters work so much. Organizations often reward effort—the amount of time people spend working—and the effort telecommuters put in can be invisible. There are lingering suspicions that people who work at home also play at home. And, when telecommuters aren't face-to-face, they don't get the informal and spontaneous recognition that's so reassuring. No wonder telecommuters worry, "Is this good enough? Am I doing enough?" When people aren't sure about the answer, they tend to work harder and longer.

There's also the danger of "out of sight, out of mind." When there's a crisis, when there's a rush, when something unexpected happens, people's natural impulse is to turn to someone they see and ask them to get involved. Being out of sight means that management has to consciously think about someone who isn't there. Many career opportunities originate in crises when leadership, decisiveness, and team-building are needed and can be demonstrated. If telecommuters, home-based consultants, and professionals have fewer opportunities to shine, will they be the first to be cut when times are tough?

Being out of sight and out of the loop means having few political allies. It is easy to create a concept or a plan by one's self. It is not possible to make it happen, to operationalize it without teammates, colleagues, supporters, and mentors. Without political allies, it becomes much more difficult to demonstrate the ability to make things happen.

E-TRUSION

About 76 million people in the United States had cell phones in 1999, 123 million carried them in 2001, and by 2003 about half of all Americans will be carrying one.[5] This is not totally good news. So many people find it so unpleasant to be near someone speaking loudly on a wireless phone that in a survey of almost 3,000 people, 60 percent said they'd rather visit the dentist.[6] In the theater the loudest and longest applause often follows the now-standard announcement, "Please turn off all cell phones." Frankly, I never wanted to know as much about total strangers as I now learn every day because people seem to really miss the wires. That's the only explanation I can think of to explain why they shout so loudly into their wireless phones.

Irish poet John O'Donohue wrote, "Email is like coming home at night after a long day and finding 70 people in your kitchen."[7]

The good news and the bad news are the same: The wonderful thing about e-communication is that we can be connected easily, with all kinds of people, wherever they are. Unfortunately, the ease of e-communication has made it a burgeoning problem as well as a solution. It now takes me at least two hours a day to read and answer my email. I need to rediscover an old truth I learned with snail mail: Most of what doesn't get answered right away...fades away.

In 1998, 66 million American employees were using

email for a total of 1 billion emails a day.[8] By 1999, the figure was 89 million people and more than 3 billion emails.[9] A study conducted by Pitney Bowes and the Institute for the Future found the typical American office worker sends and receives 201 emails, faxes, voice mails, or Post-it® notes a day. It's estimated that by 2002 there'll be 8 billion email messages sent per day, with each person receiving more than 1 thousand.

Consultant Craig Cantoni says, "One email triggers many others—not unlike an atomic chain reaction."[10] Email has become an e-annoyance. It is also a serious threat to productivity. Cantoni studied the internal communications of a major corporation and determined that half of the work-related email had "no discernible value." Nonetheless, recipients had to read it before clicking on delete.

When Information Technology (IT) blurs the boundaries between the personal and the professional, people lose control over the external demands made of them. Some people respond heroically and love it and some resent it, but everyone's stressed and some are exhausted because there isn't enough downtime or "me" time.

Fortune columnist Stewart Alsop is a venture capitalist. Besides giving him more money than most of us will ever have, his occupation gives him options that some of us could learn from. In the summer of 1999, he took a two-week vacation and despite turning on the "out of office" feature on his email, he found 700 messages in his in-box when he returned. That led him to some major discoveries. For one thing, he rediscovered the word "no." He realized that if someone he didn't know sent him an email, he really didn't have to reply.[11] That led to the insight that if he answered those 700 messages, which were all from strangers, he was letting strangers run his life. Wow! That gave him the courage to delete the emails without reading them. That gave him the strength to let the phone ring and not pick it up. That's taking control. Can the rest of us with regular jobs learn anything from that?

FAMILY UNFRIENDLY

IT has allowed alternative work arrangements and home offices to proliferate. Bravo! That provides the flexibility and control most people crave, and that's family-friendly. But eliminating the distinction between home and office, work and the personal can also be family-unfriendly.

When work is visibly the most important commitment in terms of how much time it's given and how it takes precedence, it can be extremely difficult for the people in your life to feel that they are really important. If work is the dominant passion, and much of it takes place at home, it increases the likelihood of psychological separateness despite physical closeness. *That is as family-unfriendly as it gets.*

The borderless world and IT have encouraged many people's work responsibilities to supercede their personal priorities and needs. Organizations and individuals have to recognize that demands and practices that are counter to personal needs are also detrimental to work performance. Even borderless warriors need to acknowledge the emotional and physical costs of universal accessibility and the lack of escape from work pressures.

When I address a group these days, I usually begin by asking a few questions: "Raise your hand if you're feeling significantly more pressure to keep up with your field than you did three or five years ago." Usually 100 percent of the hands go up. "Raise your hand if you have a computer at home and you work at home at night or on the weekends." That's usually another 100 percent. "Raise your hand if you get at least 25 emails a day...are working longer and harder...check in with the office when you're on vacation..."

Whether you're part of the borderless economy or not, chances are increasing that you're being impacted by the norms, the high performance requirements, the assumption of 24/7 accessibility, and the ever-rising flood of information and choices that are normal today. Although the pressures of the borderless world often increase incrementally so they don't register on our personal radar screens, the absence of total downtime has a multiplier effect. It is not surprising, therefore, that most people are feeling stressed, rarely relaxed, too close to burnout.

ENDNOTES

1. Charny, Ben, "Cell Phone Owners Paying for Spam," zdnET news Web site, November 2, 2001. *http://zdnet.com.com/2100 1105-275310.html*

2. Paulson, Amanda, "Trend Toward Telecommuting Continues," *The Christian Science Monitor csmonitor.com*, October 29, 2001 edition.

3. Paulson, Amanda, "Americans Make Space for Work, at Home," *The Christian Science Monitor csmonitor.com*, October 22, 2001 edition.

4. Owen, Jim, "A Home Business May Be the Ticket," *msn.careers* Web site, December 10, 2001.

5. Zoroya, Gregg, "Outrage Is the Order of the Day," *USA Today*, July 28, 1999, pp. D1, D2.

6. Hanrahan, Jenifer, "Survey Results Ring Clear: Limit Your Cell Phone Use," *San Diego Union-Tribune*, May 1, 1999, pp. A1, A18.

7. Cited in "Like It Or Not, You've Got Mail," *BusinessWeek*, October 4, 1999, p. 178.

8. "Messaging Today: Worldwide Trends," *Messaging Online*, March 14, 2000.

9. "Bookmarks," *Fortune*, August 16, 1999, p. 178.

10. Dauten, Dale, "The Atomic Bomb of Communications," published the week of November 8, 1998, with different titles in the *Arizona Republic, Chicago Tribune*, and many other newspapers.

11. Alsop, Stewart, "What I Learned on My Summer Vacation," *Fortune*, September 27, 1999, pp. 281–282.

2

WEB SPEED!

- EMAIL MADE WEB SPEED NORMAL
- A FIVE-YEAR PLAN IS AN EXPENSIVE ILLUSION
- IN A BORDERLESS WORLD, INNOVATION IS PLANTINUM

I was startled by phone conversations this summer after we returned from a vacation: "How are you?" the callers would ask. "Just got back from two weeks away," I replied. "Don't I know it! Took me four weeks to get on top of things when I went away for 10 days." I hadn't said anything about being swamped; the callers just knew it.

There's no downtime. Work is never finished so people use their cell phones during nonwork time and turn the time that's "wasted" into something productive. They call as they drive or shop or wait in restaurants or go to the beach on weekends.

People are very aware of the time they've "saved," but most are oblivious to their increased tension, because they multitask instead of relaxing. In July 2000, Ruben Rodriguez, a Cisco Systems Human Resources officer, attended a conference on decreasing stress because more and more company employees were complaining that they were stressed out.[1] They said the level of intensity just kept on rising. During recent meetings, Rodriguez had seen people conducting submeetings via email. Hurry! Hurry! No time to waste!

IT and the World Wide Web make accelerating change inevitable because technology, which is key to creating change, is always in a state of rapid transformation. Efforts to improve technology and increase its capabilities never cease because that's where opportunity grows the fastest.

We've gotten so used to rapid, even revolutionary change that it's hard now to feel the loss of stable conditions. It's only when people compare their lives now with what they were like a year or two or five years ago that the amount of transformation and pressure becomes tangible. Nonetheless, when markets, products, and ideas change extremely rapidly, people lose a central facet of stability, and that can be exhausting.

My book *Psychology of Women* came out in 1971 and had a shelf life of 20 years. *The Plateauing Trap*, published in 1986, was good for 10 years. 1991's *Danger in the Comfort Zone* was important for five years. *In Praise of Good Business*, which appeared in 1998, lived for three years. This book, *Seeking the Calm in the Storm*, might last 18 months. In 1999, an IBM spokesperson said an idea on the Web has a life of three months.

Before the stock markets demanded profitability, being fast, and having the advantage of being the "first mover" was perceived as better than being best. To a large extent that view still dominates. As a result, in borderless organizations, there's not much time for breathing. When you have to be fast enough to be first, life is a wind tunnel.

Water power, railroads, electricity, telephones, planes, and computers all revolutionized economies, living standards, and expectations. Some people are convinced that the Internet will equal the extraordinary effects of these earlier inventions because it interconnects people at Web speed.

When information is digital, nothing slows the speed of transmission. Information is then instantly widespread and easy to get. If the advantage goes to the fastest, in a hard-driving, fast-changing world, it's hard to be fast enough to be first. The most widely held view is that once you're in the borderless economy, you had better be moving, hurtling at breakneck speed.

INFORMATION RACES ANYWHERE!

We used to ship goods. Now we "ship" information.

The new economy is called the information economy because information has become its most important product. Today, as organizations sell services and products that make other organizations more efficient or they enable individuals to become more productive, the primary products being exchanged are ideas and data. In the era of computers, and especially since the development of the Web, there are virtually no barriers to the efficient transmission of knowledge. As a result, there are few secrets. Little can be unique for long. For a brief moment, the first one in the sandbox has no competition, lower costs, and an easier time getting branded. For a millisecond, the first to grab turf has a shot at getting the whole enchilada.

In a stable economy, planning cycles parallel the budget cycle. Once a year, management hunkers down, checks on strategy, decides on goals, and allocates resources and responsibilities. In pre-Internet stable organizations, caution prevails, pilot studies are done, and it's common to find development cycles measured in years.

In the wired borderless world of the Internet, competition morphs as fast as ideas flow, and customers have easier access to information and competitors. When venture capitalists and initial public offerings (IPOs) funded billions of dollars for Web-based ideas—ideas that could be stolen or copied in a Net nanosecond—speed was incredibly important. Before the Nasdaq crash in the spring of 2000, companies that hadn't existed a few years ago had market caps in the billions. In Web speed, life is an endless series of sprints.

George Conrades, CEO of Internet company Akamai,

says he can't plan strategy further out than 90 days because everything moves so fast.[2] In the economy of the Net, there is no long-term stability. No answer, no plan, no strategy will be the best choice for long. Strategizing, planning, trying, and deciding go on continuously because there's no time to lose. Decisions have to be made and actions have to be taken fast, without traditional analyses and pilot studies. What takes months in a stable organization is accomplished in the borderless organization in days. In turbulent times, there isn't a lot of process because process slows things down. Only the market tells you if you've got it right. This is hard ball. This is the ultimate extreme sport.

It's the power of the network that's compressing time. When 100,000 programmers, who are anywhere in the world, are developing a program that competes directly with yours, your product can become valueless in the blink of an eye. Predictions count for little when huge shifts can come from anywhere, at any time.

Speed, alone, creates a world littered with mistakes, dominated more by intuition than analysis. Haste makes waste. We all learned that. But the potential zillion-dollar payoff of speed on the Net seemed so exhilaratingly extravagant, that people couldn't afford to get hung up on a little waste. In the borderless economy, the fast eat the slow. Although deep pockets are always nice to have, having quick footwork was assumed to be even nicer.

Because the Web was so new, no one could know which

Web business models would succeed. In the second half of the 1990s, especially, there were thousands of ideas about how to organize, finance, and sell on the Web. Speed, for its own sake, was always perceived as critical.

Because the investors in financial markets are now demanding profits, they are rewarding real businesses that have real markets and competitive products and services. These are not so easily stolen or copied. That's why border-less companies are learning that speed isn't always the most important edge. Sometimes, just like in stable times, doing business right, satisfying the customer, and generating profits are key. When that's the case, the rabbit doesn't always beat the turtle, because the rabbit makes more mistakes. But the rabbit always gets there first.

Even though Wall Street now looks for quality services and products, real markets and real profits, borderless organizations have kept up the pace. They have not slowed down nor are they trying to. In a world in which communication is instantaneous and inexpensive, borderless conditions require that people always be available to make fast decisions and take immediate actions. That's why there is no slowing down, nor will there be for anyone and any organization in the borderless world.

As the world becomes increasingly borderless, increasing numbers of people will find themselves assaulted by rising demands for greater speed and innovation.

EFFICIENCY IS GOLD, INNOVATION IS PLATINUM

There is no literature that is less inspiring or more boring than the stuff written about creativity. That is really too bad, especially today when the need for effective innovation is so strong. The process of creativity remains a mystery.

Not so very long ago in the IT revolution, say from 1985 to 1995, process improvement was all the rage. That was the heyday of reengineering and quality improvement. Although process improvement programs can improve productivity dramatically, that's no longer the essence of what's happening: Web speed and the Internet changed that. As knowledge speeds, and in short order is shared, no competitive advantage lasts for long. That's why improving efficiency has become much less important than discovering and developing something customers want before they know it and before competitors have it.

The focus now is on speed, change, and creativity. The Holy Grail is "the big idea." The big idea generates an "a-ha!" response: "Yes! That's it!" It's intuitive, so there's an immediate conviction that that's the way to go. It doesn't need an explanation. People hear it and they get it.

Benchmarking is yesterday's news: Giving yourself a grade on what's already being done is looking backward. Organizations need employees who can imagine products and services that no one has thought of before. Think outside the box and push the envelope. Everyone wants to hit a creative home run, a quantum breakthrough that competitors will have trouble replicating, much less topping.

Most people can achieve baby steps, small incremental improvements. That doesn't require much in the way of perceiving and thinking very differently. But the big idea is a giant step and it requires perceiving things in a whole new way, it requires knowledge, intuition, and creativity.

Creativity has moved to center stage. It's pretty easy to identify: Like leadership, the effects are clearly visible. But like leadership, analyzing and listing the components that underlie and create creativity always seem to miss the mark. It's not the components, it's the whole wherein the magic lies. Don't play what's there, play what's not there, as the Miles Davis message goes.

Like leadership, creativity is very difficult to teach. Being creative seems to be more a matter of talent and personal courage than it is a result of experience and training. Therefore, the fastest route to innovation is identifying talented, creative people who can depart from what is and imagine what can be.

Young children are naturally creative. Unfettered by rules of what's right, kids are continuously startling us with the novelty of what they see and what they do. Unfortunately, by the time they get to kindergarten most have learned to only color within the lines.

Whereas it's hard to create creativity, it's too easy to

crush it. It is really easy to motivate people to stay safe in their confined pasts. Even when companies hire "wild ducks," they strive to tame them, to make them conform. Borderless start-ups are cauldrons of creative energy. The advantage a start-up has is it doesn't yet have a powerful hierarchy because knowledge determines power: It's too new to have strong group norms and it's too early in its development to have a powerful culture, so people are free to be themselves.

Most people who gravitate to a start-up are energized by the risk and exhilarated by the opportunity. They're ready to create a company and offer something really new. They're comfortable with uncharted territory. The most desirable achievement is to "move the needle!" as SkyStream CEO Jim Olson puts it. That means the goal is to create something so new and innovative, something akin to the Web, that could revolutionize a whole industry and maybe an economy.

As more and more countries and more and more people are wired into the Internet, more and more ideas and data will be created and exchanged. The rewards for creativity and effective innovation will grow exponentially. The amount of breakdowns and the rate of breakthroughs will both increase. Hats off to those who manage to hang in

ENDNOTES

1. della Cava, Marco R., "High-Tech Gadgets Boost Productivity–and Stress," *USA Today*, August 3, 2000, p. D10.

2. Nocera, Joseph, "The Corporation Comes Home," *Fortune*, March 6, 2000, pp. F72–F75.

3

INFORMATION TECHNOLOGY IS TOO COMPLICATED

- SIMPLE IS ELEGANT AND EFFECTIVE
- LIKE TV, IT SHOULD BE INVISIBLE
- IT PROFESSIONALS NEED TO FOCUS ON THE CUSTOMER— NOT THE TECHNOLOGY

The operating manual for my cellular phone is 83 pages long.

This "telecom instrument" has features I never imagined I would find on a telephone—a personal phone directory, a call timer, a short message service, enhanced voice privacy, and a "scratch pad." There's a wheel on the left side that controls the features, but consistent with this technology-run-amok appliance, the wheel is not called a wheel. Instead, it's called a "jog dial navigator." The manual is filled with lots of incomprehensible terms like that. I can't call the company's Help Desk because we don't have a language in common. Both the manual and the phone are so detailed and so complicated that they're user-unfriendly.

But worse is yet to come. In April 2000, Nokia introduced a wireless phone that had 32 language options, a built-in dictionary, storage capacity for 250 names and numbers, and "predictive text input"—whatever that is.

It's okay if companies give technology fans computer phones, but I don't want a telecommunication instrument. I just want a phone. I want something I can take anywhere that receives and sends calls. And maybe email. Nothing more. My ideal wireless phone doesn't need a manual.

Technology can't possible deliver on its promise to simplify our lives when, *au contraire*, it drives us crazy. Generally speaking, every technology improvement has introduced enough complexity that it requires a very steep learning curve to use. It's particularly annoying that much of the complexity is absolutely unnecessary: It's there because technical people add features just because they can. Since 80 percent of technology's features are never used, the bulk of the population, people like me who still can't program their VCRs, have to deal with impenetrable complexity for no good reason.

Technical people think it's impressive when the things they produce are overengineered and are too complicated for laymen to understand. That seems to be the preference, indeed the professional criteria of excellence for most of the people who do high-tech work. To achieve major, sustained success, technology organizations need to marry technical brilliance with easy use. That means technology has to be simple enough to be user-friendly for nontechnical people who don't relate to high-end technology.

Complexity is counterproductive when it makes it extremely difficult to figure out what really matters, or how things work. Therefore, even though some things are intrinsically complicated, all of the processes and outputs of technology, including IT, should strive to be simple and clear.

SIMPLE WORKS BEST

In November 1999, Covad was an unknown Silicon Valley company in the business of selling a commodity, high-speed access to the Net. There are many versions of the access technology and multitudes of competitors, including the deep-pocket Baby Bells. Covad's executives wanted to become visible fast in order to create a brand ahead of the pack. But it's very hard to get noticed when you're selling a commodity. Covad's executives set out to make their pitch as engaging and as simple as they could through clever television spots. They targeted "grandma" for their marketing pitch and since "grandma" wasn't interested, and didn't understand the technology, the executives decided they, too, would ignore it.

Their first television commercial opened with a "new age" yoga class. The mood was mellow, the light was warm, and the instructor was calm. Everyone was centered; not a brow was furrowed. The instructor told the class to move into the jasmine-blossom posture while he left to print out the moon charts. The scene shifted to the computer where the instructor was trying to connect to the Internet. But, no matter what he did, he couldn't get connected. As he became increasingly frustrated, enraged, and agitated, his yoga peace gave way to red-faced belligerence. The scene closed with the instructor shrieking at the computer while he pounded it with his fists.

Then the message "Faster access. Always On. The Internet as it should be" flashed across the screen. The spot closed with the Covad logo.

The commercial worked because it was funny. People remembered it. It required no explanation. And every "grandmother" could get it.

The Palm handheld computer may be the simplest technical product sold in years and it's been an extraordinary success. In his column "innovation," Charles Piller explained why he thinks the Palm is terrific.[1] The Palm, he said, does the few things he needs it to do with intuitive simplicity. It isn't cluttered up with unwanted, marginal features. And when you need to use a feature you haven't learned before, you can master it in seconds because it's designed to be simple.

The Palm delivers on its promise to plug and play, and it was designed to be error-proof. During its development, any feature that couldn't be made error-proof was eliminated. No wonder it's a smashing success: It's simple to use and easy to learn, it limits what it does, it does what it claims to do, and it only offers what it can make error-proof. That works for me.

Simple Doesn't Stay Simple

The original Palm, the Palm Pilot, was successful because of its simplicity and effectiveness. It was designed to be a personal digital assistant (PDA) and most of what it did was keep track of personal information like appointments, contacts, and phone numbers.

The Palm Pilot is simple; Palm V is useful, fast, and small; but Palm VII is different. This version added wireless communications to the PDA. Palm VII gets stock quotes from Fidelity and news from ABC, ESPN, *The Wall Street Journal*, and *USA Today*. It gives users access to the thousands of domestic and international flights that are listed in the *Official Airline Guide.* Fodor's and Zagat provide advice about where to eat. You can get driving directions and maps. There are currency converters and foreign language translators. Visa tells you where the nearest ATMs are, the Weather Channel supplies forecasts, and this Palm has its own email... but, no device works as well when it's complicated as it does when it's simple.

Convergence, or combining functions that are now in different appliances into one appliance—especially a mobile, wireless appliance—has instant appeal. The only problem, it turns out, is that when you combine functions that aren't perfected, you multiply the imperfections. Stewart Alsop, my favorite critical observer of the technical world, was thrilled to pay $500 for the new Kyocera Smartphone, which claims to integrate a phone and a PDA.[2]

To his dismay, Alsop learned the functions weren't really integrated. Convergence promises ease, but that turned out to be much too optimistic. On the one hand, the Kyocera turned out to be a rather poor phone that drops too many calls and, on the other hand, the PDA function doesn't work terribly well because it's wedded to a phone.

Our cell phones aren't great phones yet. They're not likely to become better phones when they're transmitting data and television signals.

Computer, Web, and telecommunications technologies are not invisible in the way that telephone or typewriter technologies are. The more complicated things get, the less likely they are to work well. Yet the direction of the development of technology has been toward greater complexity.

As I mentioned earlier, my digital wireless phone has an 83-page operating manual. That phone is only a phone. In the near future the phone will not be just a phone; it will be a small, mobile, wireless computer. It will access the Internet, and send and receive data, video images, and email. How many pages long will the manual be then? We now have the answer:

The manual for Japan's DoCoMo's new 3G phone is 500 pages long.[3]

It often seems that in technology, users come last. By that I mean making devices user-friendly is not usually on the technologist's radar screen. Simplicity is replaced by complexity and an arcane language understood only by the *cognoscenti* because that's what technical experts prefer. The imperative priority for such people is to advance the technology, which is far and away the biggest kick for them. Usability is a seventh...or seventieth issue. Technology companies do not normally conduct tests of the user-friendliness of their products because engineers and technology specialists really don't think about the user. They're thrilled, instead, by their innovativeness, by the creation of new technology, and by the power of the product and its new uses. Products are the progeny of their creators.

Making things worse, a lot of technical work is done in high-tech enclaves, geographic centers of technical development in which almost everyone is a technology professional. In that environment, increasing technical complexity is normal and intuitive. But technical complexity is neither normal nor intuitive for the nontechnical majority. "Techies" and "nontechies" do not share the same cortex.

Technology is sophisticated enough to make operations easy and logical. But that hasn't happened. When cell phones become portable Web browsers, the marvelously invisible software that's embedded in phones may be replaced by PC application software that's filled with glitches and is anything but invisible.

Everyone has had maddening experiences with technical quirks online. This is not only irritating, it's also very expensive. From two-thirds to three-quarters of potential Web purchasers who start the process of buying online quit and cancel the purchase because they get so irritated.[4] Potential customers don't become buyers when their experience on a Web site is frustrating because it's too hard to complete the transaction.

IT needs a revolution in its priorities. The core problem is simple but frighteningly fundamental: The computer scientists and engineers who design hardware and software usually don't know about—and couldn't care less about—what the user needs.[5] They're ignorant of the work the consumer does and the context in which the work is done.

Without knowing what a customer needs to achieve with a product and without knowing the questions the product must answer for the customer, engineers design solely on the basis of their technological expertise. The result is technology that rarely simplifies the customer's life by facilitating the outcome the customer needs.

My assistant, Helen Bloomfield, bought a copier that she

was assured would do duty as a network printer and scanner. The salesman promised that the product he sold her could perform all the functions she required. However, it took five additional visits by experienced technical installers to ask the right questions about her office network, its protocol, and how employees captured accounting information. It took these five technical visits and a long three weeks for the installers to understand how the office actually worked and to determine which additional hardware and software items would be necessary to accomplish what she had been promised could be achieved.

These problems require the simplest of solutions: Just marshal groups of people who replicate your targeted customers and watch as they use whatever you're offering. The key to success is accepting the premise that the customer is always right. If there are problems with your product own that responsibility and make the offering simpler and more user-friendly. It is heartening that in the fall of 2000, Microsoft's Jim Allchin, the boss of the Windows division, initiated monthly meetings during the design of Windows XP with the Windows User Experience Team. The goal was to identify the problems that users were likely to have with the new software and create solutions before Windows XP went into production.[6]

IT flaws derive from values that favor technology over users, speed to market over quality, and complexity over simplicity. As software has become more and more complicated, cutting-edge computer systems are failing to live up to expectations—or they're just failing.[7] Increasingly, technically sophisticated senior executives are refusing to finance major technology overhauls that involve even more complex software that is more likely to break down. That's why there's deengineering, a refusal to add features that increase complexity along with a demand that things become simpler, more effective, and less prone to errors and crashes. (Instead of using expensive personalization engines on your Web site, for example, deengineering suggests you'll get better results by having a knowledgeable, friendly, and caring person manning a Help Desk phone.)

SIMPLE WILL RETURN

There are at least two forces that encourage simplification. First, complexity in and of itself generates problems because complex systems are prone to error and breakdowns. Second, the number of technologically naïve users is exploding. This large group of people needs user-friendly hardware and software, which means fewer features and fewer functions.

> 'Tis a joy to be simple,
> 'tis a joy to be free...
> from computer complexity.[8]

Consumer discontent is leaving a mark: They're not buying. Sales of PC hardware and software are very soft. Consumers have decided that mastering new, user-unfriendly hardware and software isn't worth the amount of effort and frustration. Microsoft's efforts to make Windows XP simple to operate and crash-resistant suggests the market may have the power to generate a revolution to user-friendly technology.

"Simple sets you free," says a Fall 2000 3Com ad for Audrey, 3Com's new Web appliance that's a simple tool for exchanging email and surfing on the Internet.

While none of the new Net machines are good enough, simple enough, or cheap enough to make them a compelling alternative to the PC, progress is being made.[9] Technology, especially that which connects users to the Web, is becoming simpler and more user-friendly. A sample of products already available include:

- Gateway and America Online are selling the Gateway Connected Touch Pad, which could make Internet access as common as television sets in American homes.
- IScribe has designed software that enables doctors to write prescriptions that are easy to read on a handheld device similar to a Palm.
- IBM's NetVista is a new line of simplified computers and Internet appliances that enable easy and fast connections to the Web and other networks.

- Tellme Networks connects people to the Web by phone.
- A $350 portable tablet from Qubit Technology is a simple Internet appliance that can be attached to anything and is always on.
- MyTurn.com is selling the GlobalPC, a $299 simplified computer that does word processing, surfs the Internet, sends email, and does personal finance.
- Compaq's and Microsoft's iPAQ is an Internet appliance that gives the user access to the Web and email and costs $199.

Because these simplified products are not PCs, you can't create files or edit what you see, emails can't be sorted into folders, and you can't check bank accounts online, but these simpler, user-friendly devices do what they're intended to do without aggravation and crashing. Often, less really is more.[10]

Technology experts should step up to the enormously challenging task of "hiding" the computer. A television set, for instance, is very complicated, but we're totally unaware of its complexity because it works. Computers, software, and cell phones should be as easy to use and as reliable as the old-fashioned phone. Anything that works easily and reliably is invisible. That's the goal.

ENDNOTES

1. Piller, Charles, "Simply Put, Few High-Tech Devices Are Designed for Ease of the User," Los Angeles Times, August 9, 1999, pp. C1, C7.

2. Alsop, Stewart, "Convergence Is Still a Myth," *Fortune*, May 28, 2001, p. 46.

3. Fulford, Benjamin, and Hardy, Quentin, "Picture This," *Forbes*, October 29, 2001, p. 50.

4. Hamilton, Joan O., "A Case of Internet Itch," *BusinessWeek E.Business*, December 13, 1999, pp. 98–102.

5. Wysocki, Bernard, Jr., "Some Firms, Let Down by Costly Computers, Opt to De-Engineer," *The Wall Street Journal*, April 30, 1998, pp. A1, A6.

6. Buckman, Rebecca, "Will Windows XP Be Crowning Feat for Its Architect?," *The Wall Street Journal*, October 25, 2001, pp. A1, A3.

7. Wysocki, Bernard, Jr., *op cit.*

8. Pfeiffer, Eric W., " 'Tis a Joy to Be Simple...," *Forbes ASAP*, November 29, 1999, p. 233.

9. Wildstrom, Stephen H., "The Best Net Machine Isn't Good Enough," *BusinessWeek*, July 30, 2001, p. 19.

10. Mossberg, Walter S., "Improved Hand-Helds Still Don't Capture the Magic of Palms," *The Wall Street Journal*, May 4, 2000, p. B1.

4

DOES ANYONE CARE THAT I'M HERE?

- A SENSE OF BELONGING IS KEY TO FEELING ANCHORED
- THERE'S NO DISTANCE, TIME, OR SPACE ON THE WEB
- HUMAN EMOTIONS DETERMINE IF THE WEB'S CONNECTIONS SUCCEED

Even when I had my professor's office in the psychology department and my dean's office in the administration building, I always did my hardest work in my office at home. Four decades ago, when I was a graduate student, I became an alternative work arrangement pioneer because my kids were too young for school and we didn't have enough money for lots of babysitting. I learned to love working in solitude.

Two things made the arrangement work: The first was desperation and the second was, I belonged. I had a long-term job; in fact, I had two: one at home, and the other on campus. I knew what mattered. Priorities were clear. The brick-and-mortar world of town, university, neighborhood, and home were bound together and created a powerful sense of community. Psychologically grounded, I was free to be anywhere.

Increasingly, solid brick and mortar are giving way to continuous travel, electronic "touching," and relationships created and played out in the three-dimensional hexagon of the Web. It's the Internet that makes an infinite number of connections possible. As technology facilitates changing combinations of people, places, and organizations, how do people gain the security of feeling they belong? It is the psychological sense of belonging that enables people to feel grounded while everything keeps changing.

TECHNOLOGY MOVED FROM IMPROVING PRODUCTIVITY TO CREATING INFINITE COMBINATIONS

The Web really is different. User-friendly, it makes new kinds of relationships possible in real time between different people in different jobs in different organizations in different parts of the world. The winners in the borderless economy are those who grasp the advantages and the hazards of the Web-based plasticity of organizational structures and boundaries.

Computerization of the workplace started in the 1950s with mainframes, very large machines that were housed in special rooms and were maintained and used by people with special skills. Next, there were minicomputers, smaller and less expensive than mainframes, but big and costly compared with personal computers. PCs made it possible for millions of people to have computers at home as well as at work, and ultimately in their laps. The industry then linked PCs together using local area networks (LANs). That created a larger system of PCs, which became client–server computing, a cost-effective way to significantly increase an organization's automation capabilities.

But the client–server technology had a critical limitation, given that even within a single organization, the IT system had evolved over time and used many different kinds of software and operating systems. For client–server technology to work there had to be common operating systems and software so all the computers could communicate with each other. The task of linking computers without a common standard is terribly expensive and complicated. Thus, the number of links within an organization, much less between organizations, was severely limited.

The Internet destroyed the limits of the client–server technology because the Internet gives computing open standards and the possibility of an infinite number of connections. With a Web browser, any process or any computer can link to any other. On the Web, silos of data that were unreachable between organizations or between functions—human resources, finance, R&D, and manufacturing—can be shared, and people can collaborate and create new ways of doing business.

New software can grab information from the Web, easily add data to it, create a virtual office in which people "meet," and transform data into information. Web-based products allow people to conduct meetings online, share documents, view video clips, and chat. The Web enables real-time collaboration in very large projects with extremely complicated interactive scheduling. Many people can now work together, wherever they are.

Whether at work, at home, in a taxi, or in a hotel room, anyone can use their machine to connect with any other machine. Tightly connected permanent employees, loosely confederated cross-functional team members, nationally distributed outposts of a franchise, overseas manufacturing plants, acquired businesses, joint ventures, suppliers, and customers can all be linked. The ability to communicate and exchange information in real time and at low cost has made it far more feasible to merge operations and organizations. The result is a huge number of joint ventures, alliances, mergers, and acquisitions. Cisco Systems, for example, has successfully used mergers and acquisitions to swiftly acquire marvelous minds and products and to reshape itself and its offerings as the market has quickly changed. Cisco acquired and merged with 51 companies between 1994 and 2000. Twenty-one of those deals occurred in a single year, from March 1999 to March 2000.[1]

The user-friendly Web has made it easy to create new kinds of relationships among different people all over the world. Not many years ago, distance was linear, measured in miles and meters: The more miles or meters, the greater the limits in terms of what could be imagined. In the mental geography of the Web, there is neither distance nor time. When organizations are no longer constrained by distance and time, they can communicate, coordinate, and integrate with any other organizations. The lines between organizations are becoming blurred.

In the traditional rules of business the goal was to squeeze suppliers until they cried, keep customers ignorant so they could be gouged, and maul the competition so they withdrew from the battlefield. Now the Internet makes collaboration a source of profit because coordination reduces redundancy, thus reducing overhead. Increasingly, suppliers, customers, and even competitors are becoming partners...for a while. As business conditions shift rapidly, and as the Internet makes both combining and separating organizations reasonably inexpensive, fast, and easy, alliances, partnerships, and federations can change almost as fast.

In the pre-Internet days, we knew the rules and knew where we stood. Today, what does "partner" mean? What does "partner" mean in Germany, Mexico, Japan, Brazil, or China? Is a competitor trustworthy as a partner? Who's a customer, a competitor, a vendor, a partner, or an ally? What's my role? With whom? For how long?

With new combinations of organizations, the human factors need a lot of attention. People of very different constituencies—national origins, ethnicities, religions, values, perspectives, and assumptions about what's normal—are supposed to collaborate. IT integrates, monitors, and coordinates systems, but distance alone often leads to executives being in charge but not in control. Simultaneously, employees who are very different from those who are in charge can wonder if they count, if they belong: "Does anyone care that I'm here?"

Employees who are far from the seat of power may not identify with headquarters, may not feel a part of the larger organization, may not focus on what those in charge think is most critical, and may not really care very much about the larger organization.

MERGERS, PARTNERSHIPS, ALLIANCES, AND ACQUISITIONS

Technology makes it easy to combine widely dispersed organizations. History tells us that more often than not, that's a really poor idea. With success measured by stock prices:

- 70 percent of all international mergers fail.[2]

- In a study of 300 major mergers over a 10-year period, Mercer Management Consulting found that 57 percent of the returns of the merged companies lagged behind the average for their industries.[3]
- The number of alliances, joint ventures, and partnerships continues to grow, even though most studies report high failure rates.[4]
- Anderson Consulting Managing Partner Charles Kalmbach, Jr., reported that 61 percent of corporate partnerships are either outright failures or are just "limping along."[5]
- Multiple studies of past waves of mergers reveal that two out of every three deals did not succeed.[6] The only people who made money were shareholders of the acquired company, who received more than the company was worth.
- An analysis of U.S. companies acquired since 1997 in deals worth $15 billion or more revealed the stock of the acquirers underperformed the S&P 500 Stock Index by an average of 14 percent and underperformed their peers by four percent.[7]

Most organizational pairings make marvelous strategic sense on paper; the devil is in the emotional details.

In the early 1990s I was consulting at Rolm headquarters at a time when morale was devastated. IBM had acquired Rolm because it appeared to promise a marvelous synergy, but Rolm was now up for sale and IBM couldn't wait to get rid of it. As I listened to the Rolm executives I realized both corporations had real contempt for the key values of the other. Rolm's heroes were the mavericks who achieved megabreakthroughs in their garages after working nonstop for 90 hours. It was a gunfight-at-the-OK-corral kind of a culture. Although IBM had acquired Rolm for its innovativeness, IBMers were appalled at what they saw as a lack of systems, procedures, and discipline. The Rolmers, looking at the buttoned-down discipline of the IBM way, saw boring bureaucrats. That was a marriage made in hell and no amount of counseling could have saved it.

IT now makes it technically easy to merge operations; the increased ease of combining organizations should lead to an increase in the number of merger and acquisition failures because organizations that are anywhere usually have very different cultures and customs. Although IT facilitates the mechanics of communication, communication is only a tool for expression and explanation. Communicating does not inevitably result in solutions to the problems arising from very different cultures—from very different assumptions, philosophies, and practices—of combined organizations. Although organizations may technically combine, their cultures may not. IBM and Rolm, for example, could have talked till kingdom come, but there never would have been any meeting of minds.

Managing relationships is at least as much about hearing as it is about telling. Many difficulties in combining organizations and people are not just about differences and dis-agreements; they stem instead from a lack of respect, a lack of mutuality, an absence of chemistry, and an inability to let another entity or person win. Finding the right partners is as much about mutually held views on how to achieve and share success as it is about a strategic fit.

IT'S THE PEOPLE STUFF

John Reed, former co-chairman of CitiGroup, the result of the merger between Citicorp and Travelers, observed that

> Mergers are hard because you're trying to combine two very distinct and different cultures. Even when the need for change is obvious, when you put the culture together people behave in strange and dysfunctional ways. The Citi people became "children" who line up with me and the Travelers people align with Sandy (Sanford I. Weill, the former CEO of Traveler's Insurance). The most relevant literature to explain all this is the stuff about stepparents and blending of families. I thought we employed well-paid confident adults. That does not seem to be the case.[8]

It's the people stuff—insecurity, ego, ambition, greed, and mistrust—that's the real gravel in an organization's gears. These dangers are compounded when the boundaries of organizations are in constant movement. Then, managing relationships becomes the most critical task, which requires especially effective communication, team building, and leadership.

Most organizations, especially stable organizations, don't even fulfill the basic human needs because they don't put a lot of energy into thinking about people. In other words, most organizations don't create the circumstances and outcomes, the sense of belonging, inclusion, and recognition that increase motivation, commitment, and performance in ordinary working conditions. Those necessary conditions and outcomes are much harder to achieve in geographically dispersed organizations, especially when a lot of communication is electronic. In distanced relationships, companies have to work harder than usual to achieve just the basic universal conditions that motivate, satisfy, and energize people.

Mergers and acquisitions increase the likelihood of a dangerous combination of disparate values and perspectives that leads to mutual contempt between organizations and people. When organizations focus only on the technical feasibility and rational strategy of merging or acquiring organizations, it's easy for them to "forget" that combining organizations often results in a bad fit—a bad fit between people and the new organization and between people with very different priorities.

But best fit between people, and between people and their organization, is a necessary precondition for success. In successfully blended organizations, especially those that are linked through technology, there's mutual respect and trust because values and practices are compatible, communication is open, and people walk the talk; they do what they say. These factors are all keys to success.

Equally important, successfully merged organizations work especially hard at supplying the personalized responses that enable people to feel they count, they're valued, and they belong. In other words, someone whose opinion counts has communicated, "I know you're there and your contribution and well-being matter to me." That's not hard to supply; it just takes a little thought.

Technology can easily create links that temporarily join people and organizations, but those links of communication and data transmission and videoconferencing don't create the secure sense of belonging, connecting, and recognition that are powerful human needs. Organizations that depend solely on technical links will find that over time, most people will gravitate away from them toward arrangements or organizations that provide more permanent and secure grounding—at least for a while.

ENDNOTES

1. Thurm, Scott, "Joining the Fold," *The Wall Street Journal*, March 1, 2000, pp. A1, A12.

2. Coleman, Brian, and White, Gregory L., "In High-Tech War Rooms, Giant Is Born," *The Wall Street Journal,* November 13, 1998, pp. B1, B4 and, Ball, Jeffry, White, Joseph B., and Miller, Scott, "Grinding Gears," *The Wall Street Journal*, October 27, 2000, pp. A1, A8.

3. Ashkenas, Ronald N., DeMonaco, Lawrence J., and Francis, Suzanne C., "Making the Deal Real: How G.E. Capital Integrates Acquisitions," *Harvard Business Review*, January–February 1998, pp. 165–178.

4. Sparks, Debra, "Partners," *BusinessWeek*, October 25, 1999, pp. 106–112.

5. Sparks, *op cit.*

6. "How To Merge; after the Deal," *The Economist*, January 9, 1999, pp. 21–23.

7. Lipin, Steven, and Deogun, Nikhil, "Big Mergers of '90s Prove Disappointing to Shareholders," *The Wall Street Journal*, October 30, 2000, pp. C1, C21.

8. Reed, John, "Reflections on a Culture Clash," *Fortune*, March 20, 2000, p. 28. ©2000 Time, Inc., all rights reserved.

5 EXPERIENCE DOESN'T COUNT

- EXPERIENCE IS ONLY AS VALUABLE AS THE PRESENT IS TO THE PAST
- KNOWLEDGE IS NOW MORE VALUABLE THEN EXPERIENCE
- 3-D WEB THINKING ECLIPSES LOGICAL LINEAR THINKING

The borderless economy depends on information, on ideas, and on intellectual capital. New knowledge or a different perspective that leads to new insights is the only way to achieve competitive advantage. People who perceive differently, who innovate creatively, and who share what they know are the most valued of all assets.

That's why borderless organizations, especially, are looking for people who intuit technology, who are likely to have stunningly new ideas, extremely high energy levels, an idealistic commitment to a task, and a naïve optimism that generates the rallying cry, "We can do anything!" That usually describes younger people.

A close friend, a very successful venture capitalist in his 70s, sadly observed recently, "My experience and wisdom are not wanted." Many people who were highly successful in the stable economy, find the borderless economy bewildering, with its substantially different business models, speed, and technologies. As the newer economy expands, many of the experiences people gained in stable organizations are challenged or invalidated.

Jim Olson, CEO of the software company SkyStream Systems, invited me to give a talk to his employees. I glanced around the room and, with the exception of Jim, the average age seemed to be about 29. "My God," I thought, "Do I have anything to say that would be relevant to these people?"

As the borderless economy becomes *the* economy, the kids, adolescents, and 20-year-olds who grew up with the technology have a great advantage: They don't have to unlearn old learning.

Over-learned behaviors are extremely difficult to change. Therefore, people who have had a great deal of experience in the slower moving world of stable hierarchies may find their knowledge and skills a handicap to success today. It's hard to retrofit old ways of doing things to adapt to the online world that youngsters are so comfortable with.

As technological innovation keeps accelerating, a new

trend is impacting corporate America. Although it's most visible in borderless companies, it's also impacting stable old-economy organizations. Beginning in about 1995, people aged 40 and over became senior citizens.[1] At the Westech ECH Career Expos, which are America's largest technology-related job fairs, registration forms began to ask applicants to indicate their "professional minority status" and one of those categories is "over forty."

The key reason for the downgrading of age is the rejection of the knowledge and attitudes that were gained in stable conditions. Having lots of experience in stable organizations is often seen as a disadvantage. There's a belief that what was learned in old, established companies is not only irrelevant, but it is likely to be misleading in the borderless economy. Rejecting mature adults is also a rejection of the caution and prudence characteristic of people who've been through recessions, layoffs, and stock market crashes.

THE 3-D NERVOUS SYSTEM OF THE BRAIN AND THE WEB

People who started working with computers in early childhood are really different: They *think* in terms of what the technology can do. I wrote that sentence; I know the words. But I can't imagine what that involves.

A few years ago during a lecture I gave to a group of executives, I mentioned my ongoing frustration with my cell phone and the added insult of a manual written in incomprehensible technobabble. After the talk was finished, a woman came up to me and said, "The thing is, you went to the manual. My kids would never do that. They'd just pick up the phone and start pushing buttons." Unlike she or me, her children think from the perspective of technology.

Technologically savvy young boomers (aged 38–47 in 2002), GenXers (20–39), and GenD (Digital; 15–30) are different from most of the rest of us. We have all been trained to do logical linear thinking: from A to B to C. Effective Web thinking, which the younger generations do, is very different. Thomas Stewart of *Fortune* magazine described the Web as "an infinitely branching fractile, like a river delta" that contains a zillion opportunities and a zillion distractions in the ecological richness.[2] Fluid patterns and an infinitely branching fractile require the ability to conceptualize three-dimensionally. I call the Web a 3-D digital nervous system.

The Web is like the neurons and synapses of the brain. The synapses are the connections of the brain's cells, the neurons. With use, synaptic connections grow increasingly complex. When the neurons become interconnected, a stimulus in one part of the brain can go swiftly to other parts of the brain. Like the Web, the brain is composed of 3-D neural pathways interconnected by synapses.

There is increasing evidence that being exposed to technology at very early ages has the effect of wiring children's brains differently. When we're young, the brain is very plastic and changes constantly in response to stimulation. When we learn something new there is a significant increase in the strength of and the number of connections or synapses between the brain cells involved in that particular activity. Although this is also true for the adult brain, it is especially true for children's brains.

Today's children have many sources of neurological stimulation. Some scientists believe that the intense visual environment that many children experience with rapid-fire television editing, media saturation, and electronic games is hard-wiring children to process cognitive information very swiftly. Although there is little research on the effect of early computer use specifically, University of Iowa neurologist Antonio Damasio thinks it's likely that the kind of stimulation children experience as they interact with electronic media alters the way in which their neural circuits operate.[3]

The people who will be most successful in navigating and using the potentials of the Web are people who are not limited by linear thinking because they are able to think three-dimensionally. They will see where opportunities can be created through connections that are not visible to those whose perceptions are limited by A-to-B-to-C thinking.

Children who begin working with computers at young ages, even at two or three years old, clearly develop computer skills that swiftly eclipse those of their elders. It is easy to see that children who get involved with the world of computers at very early ages end up with a sense of comfort and ease with technology that others are unlikely to match.

But something more important than being comfortable with technology might be happening: It's plausible that when young children become facile with computers, they're developing complex neurological connections. If that's true, then the children with early technology experience may have a profound and permanent advantage over children who start later. They will have even greater advantages over people who began to learn to use computers as adults.

Many researchers have already observed that kids respond to computer games and other on-screen activities with 3-D movements that adults cannot replicate. The kids are able to synchronize the motions of their hands with the activity on screen with stunning ease. Early users of IT may be developing synaptic structures and processes that are especially suited for the effective use of computers and the Internet. If this is true, it's doubtful that even intensive training would enable adults to catch up to IT-sophisticated youngsters in terms of intuiting the technology. Indeed, some educators have begun to ask if a fundamental reason the American public schools are ineffective is that there's a growing disconnect between the way the schools teach and the way many children learn.

ABILITY OUTWEIGHS EXPERIENCE

Peter Drucker observed that not very long ago people who were in higher positions in organizations knew what their subordinates were doing because they had done the subordinate's jobs themselves.[4] Until very recently, experience created authority—and authority and power were overwhelmingly based on one's position in the organization's hierarchy. Now, experience is giving way to the greater authority of knowledge because the present and the future are increasingly different from the past.

Experience increases one's right to make decisions to the extent the present and the future are like the past. Today, the present is increasingly different from the past and the future will be even more different. In fast-changing circumstances, past experience may not only be irrelevant, it may be misleading if that experience was based on conditions that no longer exist.

Knowledge, especially in technical specialties, is changing extremely rapidly. As a result, younger people, who are usually in the lowest ranks of an organization, often have specialized knowledge and skills that no one else has or understands. Today's technical breakthrough can only be taught now, so people who graduated five years ago are unlikely to have learned that information, and people with 25 years of experience are very unlikely to know that technology. To the extent that the technical knowledge or skills are especially valuable, then hierarchically subordinate people gain a large amount of decision-making power when decisions require input based on cutting-edge technology. The traditional hierarchical pyramid is being turned on its head.

In a knowledge-based economy, relevant knowledge outweighs hierarchical status. Many stable organization managers and executives are still pretty ignorant about technology and the borderless economy. That knowledge has become a potent source of power, and it's frequently held by individual contributors who are often subordinates, consultants, and professors. Even though they're outsiders or low on the ladder, they increasingly function as partner, boss, and mentor to people who are higher in the organizational structure. What, then, is a "boss?"

When technical competence outweighs leadership experience in decision making, there is a change in who has the power to make decisions. Decision-making leadership flows from those who are less technically savvy to those who are. This often involves younger people gaining influence and authority over older, more experienced people. Young people are in charge of projects and departments that two decades ago would have been run by people in their 50s. This generation gap is huge.

The good news for adults is that in the wired world, the world keeps changing. An interesting thing is happening in the Silicon Valleys of this country: As start-ups succeed and companies grow and the markets require profitability, technically brilliant young entrepreneurs are learning that they don't have the knowledge to take the organization to the next level of growth and they don't have the maturity to resolve interpersonal conflicts or territorial factions. They lack the business experience to create structure and process and they haven't had the life experiences that develop maturity and the ability to lead and manage people. Young, inexperienced people often have trouble managing both up and down the hierarchy because they're either too assertive and controlling or too easy-going and deferential. Seasoned veterans resent taking orders from them.

Young people are the leaders of technological innovation, but they are not prepared to be the managers and executives of organizations that are larger than an informally managed, small start-up.

As organizations succeed and grow to 500 and then 1,500 or more people, youthful innovators who create start-ups are reaching out to mentors or they're hiring mature, experienced people to lead the business. Creating efficient organizational structures and effective processes is necessary when organizations need to achieve dependability and profitability. This involves very different skills—and probably personality traits—from those needed to invent an innovative technology or a new business model. Thus, wisdom, experience, and maturity are regaining some leadership ground.

ENDNOTES

1. Monk, Nina, "Finished at Forty," *Fortune*, February 1, 1999, pp. 50–66.

2. Stewart, Thomas A., "Larry Bossidy's New Role Model: Michael Dell," *Fortune*, April 12, 1999, pp. 166–168.

3. Dreazen, Tochij, and Silverman, Rachel M., "Raised in Cyberspace," *The Wall Street Journal*, January 1, 2000, p. R-47.

4. Drucker, Peter F., "The HR Imperative," The Concours Group, September 1998.

6 PRIVACY IS INVADED

- PRIVACY IS THE RIGHT TO BE LEFT ALONE
- PRIVACY IS FUNDAMENTAL TO INDIVIDUALITY
- ANY OF US CAN GET ANY AMOUNT OF INFORMATION ABOUT ANYONE

The virtual world is frighteningly amenable to unethical and illegal practices. A few years ago, one of our close friends, a very smart and astute retired professor of management at the University of California, had his identity stolen. That's the ultimate violation of a person's privacy, of the integrity of his or her being. And that theft is not hard to do.

We once bought a marvelously exciting, award-winning, extremely modern house, which we were eager to move into, but we postponed the move until the school year was over. The absolute emptiness of the new house bothered us. We needed to do something that said, "This is our house and we're going to be living here." So, we took some inexpensive furniture, a couple of rugs, three plants, and some prints from the old house to the new.

A few weeks later, we visited the new house and found someone had broken into it. Two chairs, a picture, both rugs, and the plants had been stolen. The stuff that was taken wasn't worth any money and it had no sentimental value. Nonetheless, the whole family was devastated for months. The thief had broken through the boundary of our house and had violated our private inner space. This was scary stuff.

IT'S FAR TOO EASY TO ACCESS LOTS OF INFORMATION

The Fourth Amendment to the United States Constitution says, "The right of the people to be secure in their persons, houses, papers, and effects, against unreasonable searches and seizures, shall not be violated, and no Warrants shall issue, but upon probable cause, supported by oath or affirmation, and particularly describing the place to be searched, and the persons or things to be seized."

Former FBI Director Louis Freeh told the Senate that America needs a new Fourth Amendment, one suitable for the Information Age.[1] Carnivore, the FBI's new surveillance system, ignores warrants and "reasonable cause" and can tap anyone's e-communications. Carnivore reads hundreds of thousands of messages at a time, the vast majority from innocent people, filtering them for illegal activities.[2]

Although the nets that troll for personal consumer data are huge and ubiquitous, they are so deeply underwater that they're invisible and many people are totally unaware that they're constantly being tracked. In August 2000, I received an unsolicited email from someone asking me to buy their software. The software, the email promised, would allow me to "secretly view and record everything my kids, spouse or employees have done online and off-line when I wasn't there and this fantastic new surveillance software is undetectable so no one but me would know I was recording everything that anyone did on that computer. The software records all applications loaded, all Web sites visited, all chat conversations, and all incoming and outgoing email activity." And no one would know they were being spied on but me.

Many people were reluctant to answer the questions on the long form in the 2000 U.S. Census because people have become leery; fearful that there's too much information out there about them. After all, who knows what uses data that are innocuous today might be put to in the future? There is good reason to be cautious.

Congressman Steve Horn, chairman of the House Subcommittee on Government Management, Information and Technology, commissioned a new report about the protection of people's privacy by the federal government. The results are dispiriting to say the least. The government has crucial private information about all of us—our Social Security numbers, our IRS statements, medical, employment, immigration and naturalization records, and education and family histories—the Horn Report gave the government a grade of D minus.[3] When we deal with the federal government our privacy is not secure. More than 80 percent of Americans, reported *Red Herring*, are concerned about the U.S. government's misuse of personal information. Sixty-three percent said they were reluctant to give the government detailed personal information.[4] Twice as many people said they were willing to give private information to a business than said they were willing to give that information to the government.

IT creates data and information. Whether the motives are benign or malignant, the outcome is greater surveillance and less privacy. No one is anonymous on the Web: Users are tracked through embedded numeric identifiers; through "registrations" for ostensibly free services like email; and through cookies, those unique tiny computer files that, unknown to users, are deposited on their computer's hard drive by Web sites to electronically eavesdrop and record everything you do at a site. Your Web browser passes along the fact that you used a search engine or moved from one site to another or sent an email. Email survives deletion and Internet Service Providers (ISPs) have a record of the pages that you downloaded. This vast amount of information is stored, shared, and sold.

New software does more than just collect and analyze data; artificial intelligence uses "clickstream data"—the data about where you clicked—to model each user's sequence of thoughts. Web companies are creating and selling access to huge databases that include even tiny, subtle aspects of online behavior. Engage Technologies, for example, has created a database of the behaviors and preferences of 42 million people who surf the 900 Web sites that Engage observes.[5] These data are analyzed with sophisticated profiling techniques. When a shopper who has been profiled by Engage clicks on to an e-tailer, the electronic store instantaneously receives that person's profile of interests and preferences messaged into 800 different categories. Offerings and ads can then be targeted to individuals, customized in real time to that person's demographic and psychological profile.

Customizing products, services, and ads to individuals depends on having very specific information. That, in fact, is the problem. Customizing is the rationale and ultimately the mechanism for eroding privacy.

Because the Internet started out free, that paradigm was applied to the Web. When businesses give away their information and services, they have to find another source of revenue. Information has a real dollar value. James Daly, Editor in Chief of *Business 2.0*, sounded the alarm when he wrote that among the dead and dying online companies, the personal profiles of their customers might be their last and only asset.[6] Despite promises of privacy protection, faced with huge debt it becomes very tempting for financially troubled businesses to sell their information like Boo.com, Toysmart, ToysRUs, or BabiesRUs. These troubled dot-coms sold or shared personal profiles about their customers with marketing firms.

On the Web, advertising became the prime revenue stream for many sites, but when advertisers found that banner ads were ineffective, they opted for targeted, customized messages. A message targeted to an individual naturally requires a lot of information about this person's habits, interests, and buying patterns. The sheer amount of information collected about individuals is stupefying.

The monetary value of information creates an intrinsic conflict between the individual's right to privacy and the profitability of the organization that collects the data and transforms it into even more valuable information. That's why privacy promises are made and privacy promises are broken.

IT'S MUCH TOO EASY TO GET REALLY PERSONAL INFORMATION

Data and details of people's lives used to be stored on mainframes that were hard to access. PCs and local servers in combination with the Web changed that. Imagine how freely information rushes in the geometry of the Internet. Far more privacy and secrecy has been destroyed than most people realize. And this information is for sale.

The privacy issue is not only about how much information is available about you, but also about what kinds of information are swirling about and are easily accessible. How well do I know you? Let me show you the ways...

Companies can buy or sell data taken from credit card statements, product warranty cards, or insurance reports. Organizations can learn which restaurants you prefer, what foods you eat a lot, whether or not you were hospitalized or had a car accident, which magazines you subscribe to, and where you've taken vacations.

All transactions involving credit or debit cards, all phone calls, and all dealings with any government are recorded. Database companies like Acxiom Corp. sell information about income, race, and religion, as well as names and addresses. Your choices in books, clothing, and political groups are on record, as are the drugs you're taking, your marks and class standing, what you bought, and where you browse. Employers can easily learn if you posted your résumé online. Every time you use your supermarket club card, your purchases are recorded. In 31 states genetic information can be released without your permission. In 39 states there are no privacy rights for birth defects, and in 33 there are no restrictions on divulging mental health records. Only four states protect information about abortion.[7]

Electronic tollbooths record the movements of individual cars. Closed-circuit TV cameras operate 24/7 and at least three-fourths of America's large employers monitor their employees' phone conversations, Web surfing, keystrokes, and email.[8] Employers can know how much time you spend on pornography sites, in chat rooms, browsing e-catalogs or online brokers, or gambling, and they know who sent the raunchy or hostile emails.

Many people don't realize that the personal information they provide, for instance, when they buy online, can end up on another Web site. The "anonymous" visit you made to legal sites that you'd just as soon keep under wraps—pornography, Dr. Ruth's sex advice site, hate groups, sexual perversion meeting rooms, a Gamblers Anonymous chat room, an "I Hate My Boss" message board, an AIDS information site—may not be anonymous because your name and address were supplied by another Web site.

The American Bar Association's Family Law Section has recently developed a seminar to teach divorce lawyers how to gain access to a spouse's emails, hard drives, and visits to computer sites in divorce or child custody cases.[9] Your record of online shopping could be devastating information in the hands of an adversarial divorce lawyer. The details of where you browse and linger could become public in a lawsuit. As touchy as it is in the wake of terrorism, this widespread information lends itself to entrapment as well as subpoenas.

Forbes reporter Adam Penenberg challenged Web detective Daniel Cohn to start with only his name and come up with as much information about him as he could.[10] Two days later Cohn called with Penenberg's birthdate, address, and Social Security number. "It took five minutes," Cohn said, "and I'll have the rest within the week." Using only a computer and a phone, Cohn took six days to come up with the most intimate details of Penenberg's life.

Cohn was able to tell Penenberg how much money he had in the bank, his salary, his utility bills and the amount of his rent. He got both of Penenberg's unlisted phone numbers and told him whom he called late at night. Cohn knew how much money Penenberg deposited a month and how much he spent a week. He knew the name of Penenberg's psychotherapist and how much he paid her a month. Cohn found three bank accounts that Penenberg had forgotten. Cohn knew the balances, the deposits and withdrawals, the visits to ATMs, check numbers, and the amounts and dates of Penenberg's cash management account transactions at Merrill Lynch.

Web detectives can identify your secret lover, discover hidden assets, and locate your deadbeat spouse. Your medical, financial, and driving histories are open to anyone. There appears to be no limit to the detailed information about individuals that is collected, stored, manipulated, and sold. As computers and the Web make access easy, the price of getting this information is in a free fall. Precious secrets now go for cheap and chances are very good that it is going to get a lot worse.[11] The reason this is so scary is even if you've led a blameless life, there is now swift, easy, and inexpensive access to enough personal information that it can lend itself to assertions about people based on nothing but inference.

Several years ago, Judge Robert Bork lost his chance for a seat on the Supreme Court largely because opponents to his nomination obtained Blockbuster's record of the movies he rented and others got access to what he read. From this information—and not his judicial decisions and writings—conclusions were made about his mental processes.[12] Invasion by inference is truly Orwell's 1984.

WE ARE GETTING TOO CLOSE TO BIG BROTHER

Lots of people like the customization of their online experience, but they also worry that the personal information they provide is being distributed or sold without their permission or knowledge. Until recently the positive and the negative have been weighed pretty equally. This teeter-totter balance of views about privacy was upended when tools to gather information got more powerful and less visible, and we learned how weak the government and corporate promises not to disclose, share, or sell personal information were. Right now people think the fact that the technical capacity to destroy privacy already exists outweighs the possibilities of using technology to protect privacy.

It is unnerving to think that everything you bought or searched or read or wrote or received or chose was in a database, and that information could be accessed by anyone or sold to anybody for a small sum. All of this available information makes it easy for people to steal your identity, stalk your whereabouts, abuse your credit, know your secrets, and violate the boundaries of the most fundamental thing you own: your privacy.

There is, in fact, a larger issue than the right to live without any kind of unwarranted physical or electronic scrutiny. Americans have the conceptual and constitutional right to be left alone.[13]

In a 1928 Supreme Court Decision about a wiretapping case called *Olmstead v. the United States*, Supreme Court Justice Louis Brandeis wrote:

> The protections guaranteed by the amendments (to the Constitution) is much broader in scope. The makers of our constitution undertook to secure conditions favorable to the pursuit of happiness. They recognized the significance of man's spiritual nature, of his feelings and of his intellect...They sought to protect Americans in their beliefs, their thoughts, their emotions, and their sensations. They conferred as against the government the right to be let alone—the most comprehensive of rights and the right most valued by civilized man.

The most basic right given by privacy is the right to be let alone. The right to be let alone is the right to be an individual, in control of your own decisions and actions. Even in wartime, that fundamental American right needs and deserves powerful protection.

ENDNOTES

1. Dean, Lisa S., "The Eye of the FBI," *San Diego Union-Tribune*, July 25, 2000, p. B7.

2. The tension between the right to privacy and the nation's need for greater surveillance in wartime will continue to increase during periods of conflict.

3. Kemp, Jack, "The Government and Online Privacy," *San Diego Union-Tribune*, September 27, 2000, p. B8.

4. Lamb, Elizabeth, "Graphiti," *Red Herring*, December 19, 2000, pp. 38–39.

5. McHugh, Josh, "Hall of Mirrors," *Forbes*, February 7, 2000, pp. 120–122.

6. Daly, James, "Data Dump," *Business 2.0*, September 12, 2000, p. 5.

7. Editorial, "With Patient-Data Leaks Spreading, Congress Fans the Flames," *USA Today*, July 26, 1999, p. 14A.

8. "The Surveillance Society," *The Economist*, May 1, 1999, pp. 21–23.

9. Jenkins, Holman W., Jr., "On Web Privacy, What Are We *Really* Afraid Of?," *The Wall Street Journal*, August 2, 2000, p. A23.

10. Penenberg, Adam L., "The End of Privacy," *Forbes*, November 29, 1999, pp. 182–189.

11. Green, Heather, France, Mike, Stepanek, Marcia, and Borrus, Amy, "It's Time for Rules in Wonderland," *BusinessWeek*, March 20, 2000, pp. 83–96.

12. Eger, John M., "The Precious Right to Be Left Alone," *San Diego Union-Tribune*, August 6, 2000, pp. G1, G5.

13. *Olmstead v. the United States*, 277 U.S. 438, 478 (1928).

7

FROM THE
FOXHOLE

- BASIC HUMAN NEEDS CAN-
  NOT BE IGNORED
- TOO MANY PEOPLE ARE
  FEELING CONTINUOUS ANXI-
  ETY AND CHRONIC STRESS
- STABLE ORGANIZATIONS ARE
  RARELY TRANSFORMED INTO
  BORDERLESS ONES

During the 1980s, IBM, that stalwart of capitalism, fell on hard times. Powerful competitors, including upstarts from Silicon Valley like Apple Computers and Sun Microsystems, were replacing IBM's mainframes with smaller, powerful machines, and global competition was displacing IBM from the top of the computer heap. IBM's core principle of "respect for the individual," which really meant job security for life, was in the process of becoming unsupportable. The first efforts to increase flexibility and reduce costs were early retirement packages; the corporation tried to be kind.

For many years I lectured in a large auditorium at IBM's management school in Armonk, New York. The architecture and the setting of the school were designed to express the corporation's commitment to its employees. The grounds were idyllic with paths through the woods; buildings were modern, built of fieldstone, simple and elegant at the same time. Even I, an outsider, felt enormous pride as a sort of IBMer, as I joined with management to teach in the school.

Because the problems weren't solved in one year or three, and market share and profits continued to fall, retirement packages were followed by layoffs. Employee confidence in the corporation was replaced by uncertainty and a view of a rock-solid world gave way to doubts and anxiety. As the large auditorium in Armonk filled with employees, I could almost see a cloud of brown funk arise from the bodies of the people and it stayed there, hovering and discoloring the mood, throughout the four hours of the session.

In the 1980s I had the same experience at Hewlett-Packard and AT&T and many other famed bastions of lifetime security. During the 1980s and through the 1990s, what had been unthinkable was becoming commonplace: Layoffs, job insecurity, and rising performance requirements with fewer people to do the work became ordinary.

The source of good news and the bad news is the same: Technology has made a lot of work easier and more interesting and we can communicate instantly with anyone, anywhere in the world. It is ironic that the same technology has induced levels of competition and speed and performance that contribute to anxiety and continuous stress.

Information Technology, Information Systems, and the Internet—all the drivers of the racing-speed, ultra-competitive borderless economy—are new. But people are old. Human beings have been around for an enormously long time. Over the millennia, our species developed basic human needs.

There are core needs that people need to satisfy in order for them to operate at their best. People want to belong; they want a sense of community and trust. They need some sense of stability and security. They want to be loved in intimate relationships and they want to work in organizations that are responsive to their needs. People want to be able to earn enough respect so that their opinion is sought on issues they know about or that affect them. Most people want to be recognized when they've done something significant and most people want their work to matter. We're wired to learn so it's not surprising that most adults want to keep on "growing." And people want a level playing field: They want their world to be understandable, just, and fair.

It is human nature for people to want some sense of predictability, of certainty and control. To thrive, the great majority of people need to feel they have considerable control over what's happening to them. Predictability, certainty, and control are exactly what are lost in the borderless economy. In addition to the stresses generated by ever-increasing performance requirements, a borderless world is inherently stressful because the human need for control is continuously assaulted by escalating change. For most people, that's exhausting. Prolonged exhaustion is not conducive to high performance or innovation and it's hell on wheels to relationships, physical health, and psychological well-being.

In two previous books, *Danger in the Comfort Zone* and *In Praise of Good Business*, I explained why each person has a range of risk and pressure that is comfortable for him or her.[1] Yerkes–Dodson is a simple and powerful psychological law that states that performance levels rise as fear and pressure increase from zero up to optimal levels. If fear and pressure climb higher than what is comfortable for a person, in that situation, performance declines.

In other words, when fear and pressure are either too low or too high for a person, performance is poor. People work best and are most productive when external pressures are within their individual range of comfort. Most people now live in a world where chronic pressures, uncertainties, fears, and risks are much higher than they can reasonably handle.

Despite the reality of our immersion in the borderless economy, because change on a daily basis happens pretty slowly, the majority of people unconsciously assume they have control over their life. People live their lives—they take out 30-year mortgages—as if that was true.

In the new reality, it's a funny line when we say, "A five-year plan has no purpose except to employ a strategic planner," but that's actually a very serious observation. Many of our most admired and influential business leaders have observed that they often feel like they're a small ship being tossed around in turbulent seas, or they're racing cars where there are no road signs, which makes it impossible to feel they're in control or know where they are, much less where they're going.[2]

There are, then, many reasons for people to feel stressed: Although American companies never stopped having large layoffs, even in the boom years of the 1990s, in the first quarter of 2001 more than 400,000 jobs were cut, which was almost double the peaks in the previous decade.[3] Because 75 percent of the jobs that were created between 1994 and 2000 were white-collar jobs, most of the people getting laid off are educated, experienced, skilled professionals. Managers have the harsh task of telling employee-friends that they no longer have a job while they themselves know they're high up and expensive and don't generate revenue. As hiring freezes proliferate, many people who were laid off find they have to accept a demotion—a decline in pay, in title, in decision-making responsibilities—in order to get hired somewhere else.

In organizations that have eliminated a significant percentage of jobs, the survivors are expected to do the work of those who are gone. The hours worked keep rising and desktops are never clean, making it hard to get any sense of achievement and job satisfaction.

In a long-term crisis mode, people get paranoiac. They grab territory and create alliances. They tune into rumors and chat rooms. They look busy but they don't get a lot done. Many don't take vacations, and, of those who do, the majority (83 percent in a recent study) keep in touch with the office.[4] The lack of real downtime is adding to people's mental fatigue: Too many people are never off duty because communication technologies rob them of the opportunity to be totally away from the rising demands of their universe.

Although technology's borderless economy is permanent, conditions of chronic stress are not sustainable. High levels of chronic stress debilitate people and make them unproductive, uncommitted, and uninvolved. That's unhealthy for the people and their organizations; in the long run, no society can afford that.

CHANGE EXHAUSTION

The sources of stress that have already been identified are familiar, powerful, and obvious. Another equally powerful source of stress that is less obvious although it's familiar to many, is the sense of exhaustion that arises from efforts to change that never stop and never succeed.

A borderless economy requires that businesses compete by being significantly more innovative, faster, and generally speaking, price competitive. That takes organizational flexibility, adaptability, and agility. It requires setting a course and always being ready to change it. This is a change from old values and behaviors to very new ones. Because profound change is very hard to accomplish, it is rarely totally successful.

There have been some major transformation successes: Ford Motor Company, General Electric, the United States Postal Service, and Hewlett-Packard's Test and Measurement Organization (now called Agilent) come to mind. In each case, the need for core change was self-evident; the organization clearly had a dismal future at best if the status quo persisted. And in each case an appropriate, effective, and committed leader had the helm and stayed the course. These successes have proved to be the exceptions. Most of the major change initiatives have not been successful: Some never gained momentum and others that did were replaced by a return to the old ways when good times followed crises.

Borderless organizations are different from stable organizations (see Table 7–1) because they were born after 1980, after technology had created a borderless economy, and because they have IT genes and cutting-edge, entrepreneurial cultures. The biggest difference between borderless and stable organizations is that the borderless organization was born in today's turbulent reality and does not need a core transformation of its assumptions, values, and practices. In contrast, stable organizations, especially those that had dominated their industry or had a monopoly, need to achieve an extraordinarily difficult and total transformation of their values, priorities, and operations. These are the organizations that are most likely to experience change exhaustion.

TABLE 7–1 Characteristics of Borderless and Stable Organizations

STABLE	BORDERLESS
• Calm and deliberate	• Fast, decisive
• Cautious	• Intense hum
• Quiet, comfortable	• Exciting
• Hierarchical	• Collegial
• Competitive	• Collaborative
• Professional orientation	• Business-driven
• Low- to medium-risk	• High risk
• Work is often instrumental	• Work satisfaction is critical
• Psychology of employees	• Psychology of owners
• Salaried	• Shareholders
• Good soldiers	• Entrepreneurs
• Seniority	• Meritocracy
• Report up	• Initiate
• Fun!	• Fun! And fun*
• Polite	• Direct
• Standardized	• Individualized

*Note: *Fun! means extraordinary achievement, and fun means having a good time.*

Stable organizations are usually large and old. At some point they were either very successful or, like universities, many governments, and still-regulated businesses, they never had any serious competition. Even today, there are still some stable organizations that act like they have all the time in the world. Studies, surveys, and strategies can take years to formulate and if no action follows, that's okay because there's no sense of danger. Although stable organizations do have layoffs, once the downsizing is completed the sense of crisis is replaced by complacency. Mentally, people are employees, expecting their salary and an annual increase no matter how poorly the organization is doing, and they're comfortable being told what to do and how to achieve it. Many people prefer the relatively slow pace and aspects of security that stable organizations like The Container Store chain continue to provide.

In contrast, borderless organizations are always in a hurry, either because they want to grab a market or because they never forget competition comes out of anywhere. Employees are partners and colleagues, teammates who collaborate to ensure the success of the venture—which no one takes for granted. Because of stock options, most employees feel like owners. This leads them to think in terms of the good of the business—Will this make money?—instead of the professional orientation—Is this an elegant solution? People who enjoy risk find borderless conditions, especially start-ups, fun and exciting.

Different behaviors are required in borderless organizations than in stable organizations and those behaviors reflect different values and priorities (see Table 7–2). Many behaviors or personal qualities that are common in stable organizations are barriers to success in a borderless economy. Stable organizations historically expected leaders, for example, to demonstrate authority by giving orders to their subordinates. Subordinates, in turn, did what they were told and kept on saluting. That's both slow and a waste of subordinates' knowledge and talents. It is also counterproductive because it precludes innovation and teamwork. In stable organizations that are typically hierarchical and competitive, hoarding knowledge, people, or money is an expected behavior. In borderless organizations the rule is share or you're history. Note, too, that all borderless organizational behaviors require high levels of self-confidence.

There are lots of reasons for the failure of basic transformation efforts: A change from a *stable* organization to a *borderless* organization is as fundamental as it gets. The more basic the change, the harder it is for people to grasp and accept. The more threatening the change, the more resistance is inevitable. The more years the change takes, the harder it is to sustain people's motivation to keep going. The more distant the external competitive threat, the harder it is to create a proactive change. The longer the organization was stable, and the bigger it is, the harder it is to achieve core change.

TABLE 7–2 Stable Organization Behaviors v. Borderless Organization Behaviors

STABLE	BORDERLESS
• Giving orders, telling, controlling others, requiring*	• Sharing power, listening, delegating, inspiring*
• Following procedures and rules, bureaucratic caution, learning what you're told to learn, delay decisions	• Innovative, autonomous, use judgment, entrepreneurial actions, initiate continuous learning, make decisions
• Individualistic, judge others, hoard knowledge and resources, competitive	•Collaborate, teach others, share information and resources, borderless interaction, cohesive
• Deferent, saluting up	• Creatively confront, challenge up
• Prefers sameness	• Prefers diversity

Note: *For clarity, characteristics are depicted in terms of opposites. In reality, leaders must use their judgment about when to give orders and when to share decision-making power.

The more the change is conceptual rather than concrete, the more difficult it is to pull off. It's easier, for example, to get people to use a new performance appraisal form than it is to get them to be performance driven. Change agents always talk about changing an organization's culture. The term "culture" is itself conceptual; culture is the sum of an organization's history, assumptions, and expectations. Culture involves the formal and informal values and assumptions that drive decisions and the nature of relationships. It is, therefore, not surprising that although stable organizations may change in their parts, I've never seen one become a nimble borderless organization in its whole.[5] That's why the change process rarely has a definitive end.

Some people feel that people and organizations have a finite capacity to absorb and adapt to change. If that's true, there may well be some limit to how much basic change can be achieved at any point in time. That's a warning to beware of introducing more fundamental change than people can cope with. But I don't think the amount of change that's being called for is the critical problem.

Most major organizational change efforts accomplish only partial or minimal success. As a result, many people in mature organizations are suffering from change exhaustion, the depleted outcome of successive change efforts to achieve a significant difference that either achieved only partial success or failed outright. Change exhaustion, therefore, is most likely the result of repetitive failure.

When a change initiative fails to achieve a transformation that's clearly needed, the response is usually yet another major push for change. Leaders cry out, "Let's reengineer! Restructure! Restrategize!" But the more previous efforts to change have failed, the more difficult it is for the new change process to gain credibility and champions. Success is the natural motivator and failure is the reverse:

Failure reinforces failure. Repetitive failure leads to cynicism, depression, and exhaustion and that's exactly what you find in organizations that keep trying to adapt to the new conditions of competition, turbulence, and unpredictability—but never make it.

ENDNOTES

1. Bardwick, Judith M., *Danger in the Comfort Zone*, AMACOM, New York, 1991/1994; *In Praise of Good Business*, John Wiley & Sons, New York, 1998.

2. Garten, Jeffrey E., "The Mind of the C.E.O.," *BusinessWeek*, February 5, 2001, pp. 106–110.

3. Elling, Christy, "White Collar Blues," *Fortune*, July 23, 2001, pp. 96–110.

4. Romita, Tessa, "Overworked," *Business2.com*, May 15, 2001, p. 60.

5. From reading and talking with people I have the impression that General Electric under Jack Welch may be the exception to this generalization. But as I've never consulted to GE, I've no firsthand experience to confirm that.

8

INFORMATION TECHNOLOGY IS NOT EMOTIONALLY NEUTRAL

- IT IS NOT ALIGNED WITH MANY BASIC HUMAN NEEDS
- PAY ATTENTION TO WHAT IT DOES TO THE PEOPLE WHO USE IT
- IT TRANSFORMS REALITY AND BLURS BOUNDARIES

Very few people love their computers the way they love their cars. My beloved six-year-old Lincoln Continental has 28,000 miles on it and a 100,000-mile warranty. Nothing has ever gone wrong with that car. It flies down the highway and hugs the road, its complexity invisible in its perfect high performance. I can't say that about any of our four computers.

IT has its own characteristics and they are not aligned with human nature. IT fosters working in isolation while communicating with strangers; IT accelerates endless change; IT veers toward complexity and inclusiveness, rather than focus and simplicity; IT prefers numbers and machines over people and values; IT creates a reality that's linear and cognitive and excludes the intuitive and emotional. But, IT is not your enemy and it is not going away.

Bob Phillips is a consultant who works out of his home office in Nyack, New York, while his wife Phyllis teaches school. He gets about 200 email messages a day, and when he comes back from his son's Little League game he usually has 40 or 50 new messages. He has the latest virus scanners, but twice this year his hard drive crashed, making backup to a zip disk each evening a permanent way of life. His consulting work means he has four "bosses," at least three of whom want to be able to reach him by pager or cell phone, and they frequently do. He has only met two of his current bosses in person, and hasn't been face-to-face with either of those in the past year.

Bob Phillips assumes his work is satisfactory because his clients stick around, but he has a nagging sense of unease about what they really think of him because he never sees them. Working alone in a home office, he doesn't get a chance to really explore ideas with colleagues. He's constantly in electronic communication, but because he is physically isolated, he's never certain he has really communicated. Bombarded with emails, he's also starkly alone. He's very aware that it's because he has a family that he feels he really belongs somewhere.

In a world that is increasingly unpredictable and uncontrollable, in which people feel uncertain and anxious, and in which people need more connecting and community, the fact that IT ignores the importance of emotional issues is a dangerous error of omission because emotions have become a greater driver of behavior and choices than facts and reason.

The focus on technology facilitates ignoring the human factors. The more an organization works with and communicates largely through IT, the more vital it is to pay attention to what people need. We cannot continue to think of technology and people as separate from each other. The more we do that, the less likely it is that technology will be used as effectively as it could be and the more likely it is that people will find they're more stressed than helped by the outcomes of technology. To optimize IT, it's necessary to pay attention to the human components. If they're not addressed, aspects of, or outcomes of IT may do the following:

1. Endanger trust and communication when people work in isolation with inadequate feedback and supervision in ever-changing relationships in diverse projects. The Web makes electronic communication and electronic "teams" easy to create but people do better with at least some face-to-face meetings with people they already know, respect, and trust.

2. Jeopardize commitment to the success of the organization because people don't feel they're employee-partners. Commitment to an organization follows commitment from an organization. Even in the movie industry, which aggregates people for each film, excellent work in the past is the passport to being asked to work again. Even in that sporadic industry, people do become employee-partners. The electronic freedom to constantly change partners can easily jeopardize any sense of commitment to employees from an organization.

3. Make psychological success harder to achieve because there's little or no personal recognition. Most members of management are poor at recognizing people's contributions in regular organizations where people work face-to-face. Not being there physically can make it even easier for management to ignore people, and not being noticed or appreciated is a major downer for employees. In addition, when you're physically in the place where work is being done, you're often able to achieve a sense of accomplishment because you can see where your contribution fits in. In an electronic reality it may be difficult to see the whole project and appreciate what you added.

4. Make collaboration more difficult through a lack of personal contact and no sense of being a member of

a community at work. Collaboration is easiest when everyone speaks the same language—literally and figuratively—and people, as members of a community, don't have to explain themselves. The consultant Bob Phillips, for example, describes his clients as bosses and not as colleagues. Because they rarely get together and there is no community, that's not surprising.

5. Jeopardize a sense of community through impersonal communications, too few face-to-face meetings, and a lack of shared goals and values. When I work on largely electronic projects, I find I'm still committed to doing excellent work and I want to like my electronic colleagues. But I also find that because each project's participants are assembled into a team that's short-lived, there's no commitment to the group itself. Instead of bonding into a community, we remain separate billiard balls banging around on a metaphoric green felt table.

6. Increase complexity and diffuse focus through multiple and changing work relationships and the IT professional's preference for inclusiveness and complexity. I remember when we used to put everything into 2 x 2 tables. It was really easy to see what mattered. Now we can have an infinite number of cells because the computer makes it easy to collect and massage data. With lots of cells, it's almost impossible to see anything.

7. Increase anxiety levels and stress through constant change, increasing pressure for innovation and speed, and a low project success rate. Success is the natural motivator; it gets people energized. Success is rarely achieved when the performance bar keeps rising and the basic rules keep changing. Under those conditions, people feel more stressed, more confused, and more anxious, and that's not a good grounding for great accomplishments.

IT IS NOT ALIGNED WITH HUMAN NATURE

Rob Kling and John Tillquist described a failed reengineering effort at a company they called Coast Pharmaceutical.[1] The company hired a famous consulting firm to lead the effort, and the expertise of the consultants made it extremely difficult for Coast Pharmaceutical employees to question or disagree with them. Coast's employees didn't feel they had permission to bring up what they thought were important issues, and they were afraid of voicing different views than those of the consultants because that felt politically dangerous. The employees didn't want to be labeled as uncooperative or perceived as ignorant of modern management tools.

The consultants' analysis started with preformatted

worksheets that made collecting data very efficient. But the worksheets also did something else. "Work" became processes that could be expressed in terms of time, cost, and quality. Work was now defined by the hard data that the reengineering model measured. However, the quantitative reengineering work had nothing much to do with the work experiences that mattered to the Coast employees.

The things that were really important to people were de-emphasized or ignored by the reengineering model: relationships, the intensity and pace of work, whether job security was vanishing, whether people were succeeding, and whether reengineering would make work boring. The data reengineering collected included what was quantitative and easy to get and omitted pretty much everything that mattered most to the employees. No wonder the track record of reengineering is so dreadful!

IT is not an emotionally neutral tool. It has become too intrusive in how it reshapes reality when it converts people's complex and dynamic experiences into the simple and static metrics that IT prefers.

IT clearly has a tremendous impact on productivity—but arguably, less than it could have. A preoccupation with using IT to make people more effective led to the mechanistic view that technology operates independent of the people who use it. "Hardware" and "software" are terms that describe things. And yet it has become dramatically clear that human factors ultimately determine the effectiveness of IT. The use of IT is always affected by what it does to a person's perception of and experience of his or her reality. In fact, the human factor—how the user experiences the consequences of IT—directly impacts success or failure.

The organizational changes that new IT systems and technology are meant to create—new work structures, more efficient processes, better supplier and customer linkages, global coordination, the integration of mergers and acquisitions, dispersed decision making, and continuously accessible communication—depend as much on human relationships as on technology. IT creates conditions that make the management, development, and recognition of people more important and more difficult because it links people who are geographically dispersed, who are frequently not members of a community, who may be rarely or never seen—and whose human needs must be met. More effective business solutions and processes will come when technology practices make it easier to satisfy fundamental human needs.

POROUS BOUNDARIES

The glory of technology is the rise in productivity and the decline in unemployment that the United States experienced in the second half of the 1990s.[2] Economists had long concluded that an unemployment rate of less than five percent was inflationary. The fact that the unemployment rate ranged from 3.9 percent to 4.9 percent (and 2.4 percent to 3.7 percent in San Diego)[3] without any inflation was attributed to increased employee productivity. The technology-led rise in productivity was the root cause of the better standard of living that most middle-class Americans experienced.

IT liberates many people from boring tasks, which is wonderful. IT can also make life more convenient: We can read the news on the Internet, check live Doppler radar for the weather whenever we want, avoid traffic and crowds by shopping at home in a robe, or link with business colleagues in China and have our messages translated for us.

But, like many things, there's also a darker side to technology. IT impacts individuals in ways that are both profound and threatening. Although the effect is sometimes subtle, it is also very basic. Having very clear boundaries between different things is an essential element of how people experience reality. IT takes distinctions that we took for granted, that were the bedrock of reality, and blurs them. IT can take normal distinctions like inside/outside, workplace/personal space, and ordinary reality/Web reality and make those boundaries porous. Does Internet correspondence constitute a real relationship? Are these astonishing virtual worlds we reach with a click part of our real lives?

IT can change how people experience the world. In an extreme case, the school shootings at Columbine High School in Littleton, Colorado, aggressive computer games, and a Web reality appear to have muddled the distinction between games and the real world to the two shooters for whom the games seem to have been much more vivid and satisfying than the real world.

IT is a solvent that dissolves away the boundaries between places and organizations and people. We use boundaries or conceptual categories automatically and all the time. Boundaries put new information into familiar categories that makes it easy to understand and learn as well as communicate. It's easy to see the development of this ability in young children.

When they were about two years old, my kids had a cardboard box that looked like a barn and 16 plastic animals "lived" in it. There were four species—cows, sheep, goats, and pigs; four heights—each species was different; and four colors—each animal in a species group was a different hue. It was thrilling to see the children arrange and rearrange the animals by species, by height, by species again, and then by color.

Boundaries or concepts made it possible for the children to put the animals into categories. That's the beginning of abstract thinking and it's wired into our brains. Boundaries are very fundamental building blocks for how people structure and understand their world. When clear distinctions are lost because boundaries have become fluid, people can feel uncomfortable although they may not know what is stressing them.

Why do people who live, work, and communicate

through technology need to have more attention paid to their human needs? The more people work primarily with technology, communicate primarily through technology, and are affected by technology, the more porous boundaries they experience. Technology, for instance, makes it possible to communicate with anyone, at any time, wherever they are. That can make people feel more connected or it can leave people feeling very vulnerable to the intrusion of others into their personal space. Depending on how much real-world interaction people have, the Web can foster social isolation and anonymity or it can facilitate networks of interconnected people.

Although porous boundaries are not well recognized, they can be the most profound disruption, and therefore the greatest source of stress that technology has brought into our lives, because they disturb our sense of what is normal. Novelist Barbara Kingsolver described this experience brilliantly:

> She flew forward and back and I watched her shadow in the white dust under the swing. Each time she reached the top of her arc beneath the sun, her shadow legs were transformed into the thin, curved legs of an antelope, with small rounded hooves at the bottom instead of feet. I was transfixed and horrified by the image of my sister with antelope legs. I knew it was only shadow and the angle of the sun, but still it's frightening when things you love appear suddenly changed from what you have always known.[4]

ENDNOTES

1. Kling, Rob and Tillquist, John, "Conceiving I.T.—Enabled Organizational Change," Unpublished manuscript, April 1, 1988.

2. Wessel, David, "Capital: A Green(span) Light for Productivity?" *The Wall Street Journal*, October 18, 2001, p. A1.

3. Bauder, Don, "Let's Look at San Diego's Job Figures," *San Diego Union-Tribune*, December 19, 2001, pp. C1, C3.

4. Kingsolver, Barbara, *The Poisonwood Bible*, HarperCollins Publishers, Inc., New York, 1998, p. 236.

9

INDIVIDUALS: REGAIN CONTROL!

- CONVERT VAGUE ANXIETY INTO SPECIFIC PROBLEMS AND ADDRESS THEM
- ESTABLISH PRIORITIES AND REDUCE TASK OVERLOAD
- ENGAGE MANAGEABLE RISK AND CHALLENGE AND GAIN CONFIDENCE

We now begin Part II of this book. In Part I, the goal was to identify the problems that have been created by borderlessness and the impact of Information Technology. The focus in Part II is to identify ways to help people and their organizations to manage in, and to thrive in today's challenging reality.

It is no accident that managers are getting coaches, companies are offering sabbaticals, and yoga has entered the workplace. There are onsite gyms, massages, picnic areas, and nap rooms. There are thousands of new products and new businesses to serve the needs of working people who are hopelessly too busy.

We have breakfasts in a can and one-step lunches in a bowl. Every large supermarket has a vast array of precooked food in its deli. We have traveling chefs who come to your house and prepare a week's meals. There are dog walkers, kid chauffeurs, and plant caretakers. In major cities there are concierge companies that supply people who happily climb any mountain and run any errand.

The level of stress among American adults is high and rising—about half are having trouble managing it.[1] Some solutions are pretty obvious: People need to start living within their means. Organizations need to be very clear about what's considered an acceptable work week. And organizations need to develop a new etiquette to let people know the rules about when they must be available and when it's okay to be offline and unavailable. Employees need to figure out what kinds of requirements or freedoms would be good for them at this moment in their lives.

Michelle Segal Greer used to be a division Human Resources Manager when she and Jim Olson worked at Hewlett-Packard. When Olson became President and CEO of Skystream Networks, a start-up software company, he asked Michelle to join him as vice president of Human Resources. She had two young children, so she told Jim she was willing to make the longer commute, but there was absolutely no way she could commit to very long, uncertain, or irregular hours. "That's fine with me," he said, "I've got young kids, too."[2]

A common source of stress stems from the fact that it's getting harder and harder to get away from work. Our high-tech tools, the Palms, pagers, cell phones, and laptops, all the things that keep us connected, boost our productivity—and our stress. We bring these tools on vacation, if we even take one. Most people need to draw a line between work and home. They need to take a real time-out, have some fun, and connect with the people they care about.

There are lots of things that people can do to make themselves feel better and they need to find what works for them.[3] People need, for example, to find activities that bring a grin to their faces; most people should take vacations and on vacation, disconnect. People should explore ways that help them to recharge. They can join a club, go to church, learn a skill, have a hobby, master meditation, or practice yoga.

I love hatha yoga. It's the exercise form of yoga and it makes you feel great. I've been practicing yoga for 31 years and I'm pretty good at it. But, like having a massage, making new friends, or having a great vacation, it makes you feel better *for a while*. Yoga, massages, vacations, or new friends don't address and cannot change the basic reasons why people are so stressed.

The fundamental reasons why most people are too stressed are first, they're experiencing anxiety, which is a vague sense of dread or uncertainty about what's going to happen. Second, the majority of Americans have much too much to do because the demands made by their work and personal universes keep rising: Their to-do lists keep growing faster than tasks can be accomplished. And last-ly, thriving in a borderless world requires a lot of autono-my, initiative, and flexibility. But many people don't have enough self-confidence to be self-directed, proactive, and adaptable, especially in tumultuous conditions.

To regain a sense of having control in our harried lives, we need to reduce anxiety, reduce overload, and gain confidence.

ANXIETY

In 1999, George Bell, then CEO of Excite, tried to explain his profound sense of weariness to former Internet pioneer and CEO Michael Wolff. Bell said:

It's not just the airplanes. It's not just raising money—endless amounts of money. It's not just looking at a vast pay-roll every other week at a company that is not able to reli-ably support itself. It's not just the uncertainty. It's not just the 24/7 business schedule. It's the acceleration. Your job is to transform—and to be transformed. To be able to with-stand some speeded-up evolutionary process. And, of course, to be one of the evolutionary survivors...I've lost the capacity to let my guard down.[4]

Bell was burned out. Burnout is a state of exhaustion, the result of prolonged stress and anxiety. Burnout has become more common over the past decade as the borderless economy led to unrelieved pressure; shorter and shorter time frames; and hugely expanded work days, weeks, and months. Burnout results from a long-term persistent feeling that you've lost control over what's happening to you. Instead of feeling in control, you feel controlled by everyone else's demands and needs, pushed by events and commitments without choices, unable to say "no."

When people are feeling very anxious, they desperately want to feel they can trust other people, and that requires that they believe they're being told the truth. At work that means that management, especially, must walk the talk. It is crucial that management does what it says it will. Anxious people require structure and clarity. Tasks and goals need to be specific, priorities need to be clear, and deadlines for subparts of a project as well as the completed task need to be supplied. Because anxious people need specific goals, priorities, rules, and deadlines, when management doesn't supply them, employees must ask for them.

The intrinsic unpredictability of the borderless world lends itself to increased anxiety, *a vague feeling of dread or threat.* Because anxiety doesn't have a clear shape, it is very different from fear, which is specific. Anxiety is a very powerful negative emotion and its cumulative power arises from its vagueness because we can't put our arms around a shadow or a cloud.

The events of September 11, 2001 scared many people. It was appropriate to be afraid of more terrorist attacks, especially if you lived in New York, Washington, DC, or anywhere else that included logical symbolic or military targets. But from a psychological point of view, the power of September 11 was not that people got fearful. Rather, the assault on the World Trade Center especially, caused many psychologically normal people to become profoundly anxious, preoccupied for a few days or weeks with unanswerable questions: "Am I going to die? What is going to happen to me?"

Anxiety is expressed in the cry, "What is going to happen to me?" which is very different from a fear like, "If I don't have this operation, I could die!" In the real world, no one knows and no one *can* know what is going to happen to them or anyone else. "What is going to happen to me?" is a futile question because it has no answer, which is why most people, most of the time, don't dwell on questions like that. Because anxiety generates questions without answers, anxiety generates more anxiety, which is very destructive to people's well-being.

To reduce *normal* anxiety levels like those generated by the terrorist attacks on September 11, vague anxiety or dread must be converted into specific fears or problems.[5] Once a vague sense of foreboding has become a specific fear or problem, people can start to address the issue, create plans, and take action. They can *do* something. Just taking action starts to reinstate some sense of personal control. "If I don't have this operation..." becomes an action plan: How do I find an outstanding surgeon? Which hospitals have a great track record for this kind of surgery? What are my options?

At work today, many people are appropriately anxious about being laid off and their thoughts are filled with dread: "Our department has had only a couple of layoffs so we're next, I'm sure of it. And I'm a manager so I'm a cost and an expensive one so I'm probably at the top of the list. My boss has been avoiding me and I know that means something. God, I'm scared."

Although these anxious thoughts are normal, they're not helpful. Dread must be converted to items that can become actions: "I'd better ask my manager what she knows or what she thinks. If she thinks I could lose my job, my wife Alice and I'd better cut expenses. I'd better get my Rolodex up to date and start networking. I should probably be doing that anyway. Are there some skills I need to upgrade? Would Alice go back to work? What options do I have?"

Feeling anxious is the epitome of feeling you have no control over what is happening to you. Anxiety begets more anxiety because we can't solve problems that are vague and nonspecific. To master anxiety, it's necessary to convert whatever is threatening and amorphous into something real and specific. Just transforming vague anxiety into specific issues contributes to regaining a sense of having control.

When anxiety has been transformed into definite fears or issues, there is a real possibility that they can be addressed and solved.

OVERLOAD

Many years ago when I had a shiny new Ph.D. and three kids under the age of six, I became a half-time lecturer in the Psychology Department of the University of Michigan. It was the largest psychology department in the country at the time, but there was only one woman on the faculty who held a regular appointment as a professor.[6] All the other women on the faculty had nonregular positions, such as lecturers.

With ambitions to become a professor, I went to the chairman of the department and asked him how the faculty were evaluated. "You'll be graded on three things," he said, "teaching, community or professional service, and research and publications." "Which is most important?" I asked. "They're all equal," he said.

He lied. It took me a while to learn that at a research university like Michigan, the most important factor you're judged on is the quality of your research and publications because that's the business of that business. Teaching is of barely second place importance in that kind of university, and service is a very, very distant third.

When I knew what really mattered, it was easy to decide

on priorities: As a full-time mom and a part-time career woman, I would devote the greatest amount of my work time to research and writing. Next, I'd work to make my classes exciting because I'd teach what was really cutting edge. And I would say, "Thanks, but no," to any invitations to sit on department, university, or national committees until all my children were in school for a full day.

We're also dominated by the demand for speed: Messages we once would have taken a week or two to answer, if they got answered at all, are now answered immediately because they're email. We don't notice that speed has become the driver of what we do, and speed has created compressed time frames that add to our stress. We've forgotten that lots of messages don't need an answer and if we answer every message, we keep adding to our workload.

The most important thing to remember is that everything is not equally important. To reduce life's workload, people have to set priorities. It's like inboxes: One box is for materials that require immediate attention; one box holds things that need to be done, but there's no particular hurry; and a third box is for things you'll get to eventually...maybe. Creating priorities means creating categories of degrees of importance, and that limits how many items must be tended to immediately. Setting priorities gives people a sense of control because when you prioritize you are less controlled by tasks.

Setting priorities helped me realize what I really had to

do—and what I didn't need to do. It let me know what I had to do marvelously well, what could be okay, and which commitments could be ignored. Setting priorities and discovering that "no" is a really useful tool is a way to reduce task overload.

Creating priorities and looking good have become especially important and useful to people wherever downsizing has occurred because the people who are still employed are expected to do the work of the people who are gone. But, some tasks are more important than others and those require a commitment of time and a commitment to excellence. Other tasks can be okay—and that's okay. The trick is to strategize: Differentiate on the basis of importance among aspects of work while continuing to look involved, enthusiastic, and committed.

Americans are tired. Employees in the United States put in more hours and have less vacation time than people in any other advanced industrial nation.[7] The average American works the equivalent of eight weeks a year longer than the average Western European. More than 37 percent of us put in more than 50 hours a week. In more than half of American couples, both partners come home from work after 7 p.m. and face all the tasks and responsibilities of their second job, the domestic one. Stress rises when there are no limits to the demands made on people at work and at home. Our days are fully scheduled and the schedule can't be met without Herculean efforts.

It is psychologically unhealthy when there are no boundaries on what people are expected to do, no limits on how much people are expected to pay attention to and be responsible for. That's why reducing overload also involves delegating, or not always being the person who does everything.

Huge amounts of information are widely available and easily accessible, especially on the Web. With information readily available, there's an increasing assumption that people are responsible for getting it and using it. The value of many intermediaries, like travel agents, seems to be in decline: It's so easy to make plane reservations, get electronic tickets, and book hotel rooms that many people do it themselves.

A recent experience, however, suggests that travel agents must not disappear! My husband and I recently took a trip to France, pursuing great food in Paris and Burgundy. As the person who was responsible for planning the trip, I read, surfed, highlighted, summarized, compared—and made reservations. Because it was summer, I chose air-conditioned hotels, but couldn't find one in Dijon. I settled for a three-star hotel that was described in four recent guidebooks as "an extremely charming place," a converted 17th-century inn.

The exterior of the hotel was pleasant, but "charming" would be an exaggeration. The man who registered us was gracious, but not charming enough to help with the luggage.

The sitting and dining area was pleasant, but not enough to be charming. The elevator was too small to hold the two of us. The room was awful. The furniture was depressing. But that was nothing compared with the heat.

It was really hot in August and our tiny room had one tiny window that faced a totally enclosed courtyard, designed to protect 17th-century travelers from bandits. There wasn't a breath of air. We both took five cold showers in two hours. When it was time to try and sleep we propped the door to the hallway open to catch any breeze, hoping we wouldn't be robbed or killed.

The next morning we walked around Dijon and saw a large billboard that announced three brand new, air-conditioned hotels. Even though my information had been current, it wasn't right. A travel agent would have had better information because he or she would have access to information that I didn't. That incident made me realize that I don't want to be responsible for knowing everything about everything. As much as I learned in planning the trip to France, I didn't know enough. I should have turned to an expert.

Even more important than getting the best information, I realized that in order to have some control in my life, I have to be able to choose what I'm responsible for knowing. Huge amounts of accessible information don't make me free. Instead, they add to what I'm supposed to know and do. We have to be able to *not* know something about everything.

Only then are we free from the responsibility of doing everything. A little ignorance can create a calm haven.

To regain a sense of having some control over what happens to us in a borderless world, we have to change anxiety—vague feelings of dread or panic—into specific issues we can do something about. To reduce our sense of overload, we need to delegate when that's the right thing to do. And we need to know what really matters so we can set priorities and limit how much we have to do now! And, lastly, to have a sense of control in unpredictable and demanding conditions, we need to develop enough confidence such that change is more exciting than it is scary. Confidence is the attribute that liberates us from fear.

GROW IN CONFIDENCE

A borderless world is intrinsically risky and unpredictable. Thriving in borderless conditions requires high levels of confidence because confidence increases people's ability to handle risk and be comfortable with change.

It takes confidence to behave in the ways that borderless conditions require; to make fast decisions and act on them, to share resources and knowledge, to initiate instead of wait for orders, and to be direct and disagree with bosses and colleagues when you think you're right. People don't share power and knowledge, hand off decisions, prefer spirited debate, or delegate to others unless they are very confident.

Confidence is *the liberating quality* because it is the only condition that frees us from the fear of failing, the fear of being powerless or insignificant...or of being laid off. It's no fun to lose your job. But confident and nonconfident people react differently to being laid off. Nonconfident people tend to respond to the possibility or actuality of losing their job with counterproductive responses: They panic, they freeze, or they get very depressed. Confident people are more likely to anticipate the possibility and plan for it. Nonconfident people are likely to see only a bleak future and grab for a job, even if its prospects are poor. Confident people are not likely to panic because they view the economy as cyclic and they're psychologically better able to wait and be selective about what they'll do next. Confident people's responses tend to be constructive and adaptive, whereas nonconfident people's reactions are not. As the world grows more borderless and the economy more turbulent and Darwinian, the more critical it is for people to be confident.

Confidence increases when people succeed in mastering tasks they haven't mastered before, the task is of medium difficulty for them, and the outcome really matters. Nothing succeeds like success. Success is the natural motivator: It increases confidence and energizes enthusiasm.

Confidence means someone is willing to handle risk, and it is the result of striving, stretching, and (usually) succeeding. To gain confidence, people need to succeed in hitting increasing performance goals in circumstances in which there's some risk. Risk means something significantly different happens to you when you succeed and when you don't. Hitting stretch targets where there is no risk, where nothing much different happens to you if you succeed or if you fail, does not result in increased confidence because confidence is about being able to handle risk.

Too much security or prolonged protection from risk leaves people unable to handle it. It is ironic that the protection from risk that many people seek and gain in stable conditions leave those people without the experience and skills, the resilience, and the confidence to cope with borderless conditions.

Today, fleeing from challenges and trying to stay safe is a very poor blueprint for managing in reality. People need to resist the temptation to "stay safe," to continue doing what they've already learned because it's easy and they never make mistakes. Moving toward manageable challenge and risk in order to successfully grapple with difficulty and develop self-confidence is probably the single most important responsibility we each have for ourselves. In borderless conditions, most people need to keep pushing themselves beyond the envelope of their comfort zone.

The development of confidence is encouraged when managers, teachers, and parents "manage to success." When people manage to success, they want others to succeed and grow confident. This is the opposite of "managing to fear," where the goal is to instill enough fear so that obedience is the result. Confidence cannot develop where fear is the motivator.

Confidence requires earning success; failure does not develop confidence. Therefore, the difficulty of people's challenges must increase in small enough steps that success is still likely. As confidence increases, the level of risk and the difficulty of the tasks which are comfortable, rise in larger and larger amounts. As confidence rises, the process becomes self-initiating: Fun for confident people is grappling with a tough task when the odds are long and the outcome really matters.

To rebuild a sense of control and increase confidence, people should take an active role in having manageable challenges and risk in their lives. Toward that end they need to ask the organizations in which they work, play, and learn to collaborate with them in creating stretch challenges that really matter. At the same time, parents, professors, teachers, supervisors, managers, scout masters, drill sergeants— anyone who has responsibility for setting goals and evaluating people's performance—needs to learn how to manage to success.

With individual initiative and institutional collaboration, most people can and will reduce their anxiety level, gain more control over their workload, and develop the confidence that will allow them to prefer the excitement of the borderless world over the predictability of stable conditions.

ENDNOTES

1. Higble, Andrea, "When Stress Calls," *San Diego Union-Tribune*, March 12, 2001, pp. C1, C2.

2. Personal communication, June 2000.

3. Sometimes the issues are more clinical and thus more serious. People with stress-sensitive or stress-causing illness, including anxiety or panic attacks, addictions, or depression, could benefit from psychotherapy.

4. Wolff, Michael, "The E Decade," New York, December 6, 1999, pp. 34–41.

5. I'm talking about nonpathological levels of anxiety that can be reduced in the ways described here. Pathological levels of anxiety, like phobias, need psychotherapy.

6. A regular appointment is on the academic ladder of assistant, associate, and full professor. That ladder leads to academic tenure. Nonregular appointments are not eligible for tenure.

7. Lardner, James, "World-Class Workaholics," *U.S. News and World Report*, December 20, 1999, pp. 42–53.

10

INDIVIDUALS: ARE YOU A FORD OR A FERRARI?

- FORDS WANT SECURITY, RAISES, AND PROMOTIONS; FERRARIS WANT TURBULENCE, AND A CHANCE TO WORK ON THE "NEXT BIG THING"
- MANAGEMENT MUST LEARN TO UNDERSTAND THE MOTIVES AND PRIORITIES OF FERRARIS
- FERRARIS MAY REVITALIZE THE AMERICAN TRADITION OF INDIVIDUALISM

For the first time since the Great Depression of 1929, America has a group of people who bear no depression-era scars. Though small in numbers—they're a minority within the generations of younger boomers, GenX, and GenD[1]—they're extremely important. I call them Ferraris and they are significantly different from the majority of people who are Fords. There are many, many more Fords than Ferraris, and the two groups have almost nothing in common. Most members of management are not Ferraris and they don't understand what motivates this group.

Fords prefer a mutual compact between themselves and their organization of long-term security and loyalty. The fear of insecurity that drove their parents and grandparents to seek security above everything else remains very relevant to them. But Ferraris are very different: They prefer risk. Ferraris tend to stay with an organization only as long as there's a really good answer to, "What's in this for me?" To be satisfied and fully engaged in an enterprise, Ferraris require the challenge and excitement of moving at speeds where the margin of control is very narrow and the need for sharp reflexes is unyielding.

Ferraris are the natural leaders in a borderless world because they're vastly more comfortable in turbulent and risky conditions than Fords and they are much more engrossed by challenging conditions than stable ones. My husband, Allen Armstrong, was a captain in the Coast Guard and a master mariner, licensed to be in command of any size ship in any waters. "As long as you have a sturdy ship beneath you," he says, "there's nothing as wonderful as being in a great storm at sea."

Do you prefer security or risk? Every person has to assess what's most important or valuable to him or her at this time in life.[2] Would you feel better knowing your company has a no-layoff policy and your job and salary are pretty safe, or would you rather go to work at a start-up and hope stock options would someday make you rich? Are you willing to work very long hours, sometimes seven days a week, or is it really important that you work reasonable hours and have a flexible work arrangement? Is it critical to you that you get to work on your own ideas and are responsible for a whole project or would you feel more comfortable if your boss told you what to do and the responsibility for the project was shared with many other people?

Each of us has to honestly answer the question, "Are you a Ford or a Ferrari?" because we need to work in conditions that suit us, in which we're more likely to flourish and contribute.[2] People need to find the circumstances of risk or security, stability or change, autonomy or hierarchy in which they're comfortable and can use their strengths, rather than try to avoid their weaknesses. To succeed, people need to fit in to the values, styles, and expectations of their organization.

Most Ferraris are members of borderless organizations or they're self-employed. The majority are young professionals, usually between 20 and 40 years old, who take the digital world for granted and are confident that their knowledge and talent is the organization's key resource.

Ferraris assume they'll participate in making decisions as soon as they're on board and they expect to have a shot at leading based on what they know. They're far more interested in doing creative and challenging work than they are in managing other people, so climbing up the corporate ladder isn't very important to them. They prefer autonomy and the chance to be creative, although they're accustomed to teamwork.

Ferraris are not without faults: It is not uncommon for some of them to be arrogant about their technical abilities, and inflated egos and rampant narcissism are not unusual. Some who are arrogant about their technical abilities feel free to challenge others but often bridle when they are challenged. Physicists, mathematicians, computer scientists, and brilliant hackers are usually introverted and solitary people.[3] As a group, they are technically superb and interpersonally inept. It's good that most of them are not interested in managing others because this is not the best pool in which to fish for marvelous management.

Ferraris romanticize the heroics of hard work. It is really appealing, perhaps thrilling, to see yourself as a big winner who thrives on risk. It's exciting to be a superperson, someone who can fly cross-country for a two-hour meeting, fly right back, and be in the office at 6 a.m. sharp. When macho is idealized, it's an ego trip to complain and boast about your 100-hour work week and how you catnapped under your desk. It's heady stuff to see yourself as the keystone of the enterprise.

But the assets of Ferraris far outweigh their liabilities. Ferraris are so confident about their work skills that they're comfortable with levels of risk that are much too high for most people. It could be argued that they don't experience high levels of work-related risk as risky because they have no fears about economic security. They view traditional job security and a lifetime career with one or very few employers as stifling and boring. Understandably, some of these people are addicted to adrenaline; they need the highs of tremendous challenge and change. Ferraris are risk creators; Fords are security seekers.

Although there are relatively few Ferraris, their importance is disproportionately high to their numbers. In a world of permanent turbulence and change, the great strength of Ferraris is that they *prefer* conditions of rapid change, excitement, and required high performance. The majority of leaders in the borderless world will be Ferraris because there's a natural fit between people who are risk creators and a reality that is very risky. In borderless conditions, Ferraris are incredibly valuable. To attract them and to keep them for even a while, we have to understand them and give them what they want.

FERRARIS WANT!

Ferraris are usually so different from Fords that management, which is often largely composed of Fords, finds their motives and priorities inexplicable. The working conditions and rewards that Fords want most—security, raises, recognition, and promotions—are not of interest to Ferraris. Organizations that want to attract and keep Ferraris will have to meet their requirements.

Ferraris are willing to commit to extremely hard work as long as the organization:

- treats them as individuals;
- gives them the freedom to initiate, make decisions, and lead;
- doesn't slow them down;
- gives them the chance to learn and innovate;
- gives them the opportunity to work with super sharp people;
- lets them do important cutting-edge work;
- buys them the latest technology toys;
- has a culture in which achievement determines status;
- is fair and tells it like it is;
- creates bonds that connect everyone;
- is filled with excitement and the fun! of achievement;
- is a place where people play;
- might be a place in which they'll earn lots of money.

Ferraris are not grateful because they have a job. Confident and independent, they're mentally free to join or to leave organizations—on their terms. Attracting and satisfying them takes an environment that contains all of these elements.

When these requirements are clustered we end up with four key outcomes or conditions that are the highest priorities for Ferraris:

1. People who join borderless organizations, especially start-ups, want to create something so new and rev-

olutionary, that's so far beyond the ordinary, that it "moves the needle."

2. If they make major contributions and the company succeeds, they want a significant level of compensation.

3. Ferraris insist on being treated as individuals, which involves customizing their work experiences.

4. They want to play, for fun and as a way to connect with the people they work with.

MOVE THE NEEDLE!

If you ask anyone, "What's most important to you at work?" Nine times out of 10 the first thing they'll say is, "Challenge. I want to keep learning and stretching." That's baby steps in comparison with moving the needle which is achieved only by giant steps of innovation and impact.

"We are changing the world." (Kim Polese, cofounder of Marimba, Inc.)[4]

"When I project 5 or 10 years down the road, I want to look back and realize that I was at the creation of something great." (Marc Andreeson, chairman of the board of Loudcloud and cocreator of Mosaic, which became Netscape)[5]

"That's mine—I wrote that—and it's sitting on a million desktops." (That's the hope of Chris Strahorn, a 24-year-old programmer at the San Francisco start-up Tomorrow Factory.)[6]

Before Silicon Valley fell into recession in 2000 and 2001, Ferraris routinely moved from one organization to another, gravitating to the thick of what was important and happening. They wanted a shot at working on the next big thing, the thing that would revolutionize a company, an industry, the world. That's why they gravitate to the company of brilliant people. They go wherever there's a good chance of coming up with something stunningly new.

Although Ferraris certainly gravitate to greater financial opportunities, the biggest draw for the most innovative of them is to destroy, create, and change, and they want to do it fast. They move to where the best people, the earth-shakers, are congregating. They're looking to make giant steps, a major breakthrough, preferably in a company that's still small, where an individual's efforts can make a whale of a difference. The Microsofts of this world are too large to attract or retain the most entrepreneurial of these people.

MAKE ME RICH!

Today, success is still partly psychological: I moved the needle! But to an unprecedented extent, especially for people in the borderless economy, success became largely financial. What is new—and this is not news—is that many people, especially younger ones in start-ups, expect—or expected—to gain millions of dollars in just a few years of hard work. Even young people personally know others, who are basically just like them, who became millionaires.

Many people know others who were simply in the right place at the right time. I know a young man who joined Excite before it went public, whose options cost him 25 cents, he exercised them when the stock hit $100. My husband's brother-in-law knows a secretary who joined a fledgling company and she's now worth $50 million because that firm was America Online. San Diego has hundreds of QUALCOMM millionaires. Many of them are competent—but not outstanding—managers and professionals, and their options are currently worth between $1 million and $5 million dollars. The crux of the matter is that the possibility of becoming a millionaire moved from the rarefied air of Tiffany's to the more ordinary venue of Macy's.

Gurus, consultants, and psychologists have long asserted that people don't work for money. How naïve can "experts" be? The idea that money doesn't motivate people is based on three things:

1. Given the option of well-paid boring work or reasonably paid fascinating work, people prefer to do the work that fascinates them.

2. There are lots of data from psychological studies using university students who were paid a large sum

for poor students—$5 an hour—to do boring tasks. The data revealed—surprise!— that the students were bored.

3. Regular bonuses don't create a lot of motivation. It is hardly surprising that corporate bonuses that average $83 a month after taxes do not generate a lot of goosebumps.

Does anyone notice the piddly amounts of money? Borderless companies, especially pre-IPO start-ups and their stock options changed all that.[7]

Especially in the second half of the 1990s, success involved amounts of money that had been unimaginable just a few years before. Options, in particular, sometimes made people so rich that they were (and are) free to make all the choices they can imagine in a lifetime. That is a transformational amount of money; it changes your life. While founders sometimes became billionaires, many employees became millionaires. It's as though everyone in the neighborhood won the lottery. Would that kind of money motivate people? Does the moon rise at night?

Organizations that are under enormous pressure to attract and keep Ferraris still need to take the possibility of large amounts of money seriously. The motive to get rich became very important to an unusually large number of people because the possibility was very real. Only time and the future state of the economy will reveal how permanent that goal became for most Ferraris and a considerable number of Fords.

TREAT ME AS AN INDIVIDUAL!

"Amazon.com knows what books I like, L.L. Bean's Web site knows my clothing sizes and preferences, Neiman-Marcus calls me when my favorite designer's clothing is going on sale, and the art gallery in San Francisco sends me an email when an artist they know I like or think I might like is going to be in their new show, so how come my boss doesn't know anything about me?"

Customizing the customer's experience became a mantra of the Web age. Ferraris are very likely to make customizing the employee's experience of equal importance.

The fact that Ferraris who are young boomers (aged 38–47 in 2002), GenXers (20–37 years old), and GenDers (15–30 years old) who join borderless organizations are unwilling to wear suits is a symbolic expression that they are not willing to be suits. "I look the way I like, I wear what I please, I say what I think, and I do what's fun." "I, me," and "my" are important words to them. This population wants ownership; they want to work on their ideas. They want "my life, my choices, my decisions, my responsibilities."

They're unwilling to be caged by requirements that force narrow conformity. That makes them far less predictable than older generations and most of the other young people who prefer stable organizations.

Ferraris feel free to be idiosyncratic; they frequently have their own definitions of success. A very ambitious, seemingly driven executive of a dot-com told me, "If things work out financially like I think they might, I think it would be fun to stay home and raise my kids for a while." And that—to my total surprise—is exactly what he did!

The borderless economy requires extraordinary insight, dedication, and creativity to win. These are qualities of individuals. In order to satisfy the requirements of Ferraris, and enable insight, dedication, and creativity to flourish, management needs to stop treating people like identical widgets and move toward a perspective that perceives, encourages, and rewards individuals rather than groups or generations.

LET'S HAVE FUN!

Ferraris in borderless organizations put fun! first. That's moving the needle. But, they also want fun; they want to play with the people with whom they work. For them, the dividing line between work and play is permeable, which is pretty extraordinary. If you play with people it means you enjoy them, you trust them, and you see them as friends and colleagues rather than as enemies and competitors. That's very different from what you find in most large, stable organizations in which there's an unstated but never-ending competition between people who are elbowing each other, vying for recognition and promotions.

There is also a serious side to the fun in borderless companies. Borderless conditions are exhausting as well as exhilarating. They're stressful as well as successful. They're out of control as well as in the money. When conditions are tense, people try to make themselves feel better. They turn to commitments that are supportive like their families and they may try to create a sense of fun and of belonging within a community at work.

The basis for having fun at work is trust and having a sense of membership. In addition to "I, me, and mine," "*us*" has to be a vital part of the enterprise. People need to feel they're part of a community and within the community, that they're accepted and connected. That's easiest to achieve in a small start-up. Size alone generates anonymity and a lack of community which makes it very hard for people to have a sense of trust or a sense of belonging. Large organizations need to give people the experience of being part of small communities: That could include membership in permanent teams, small group projects, or long-term committee assignments.

The really good news is there are Ferraris, people who are really energized, who really thrive in the high-risk, fast-paced, 24/7 borderless world. Ferraris are so confident that most of the time risk, turbulence, and unpredictability contribute to a sense of excitement and even exhilaration. Organizations that want to attract this group must remember that Ferraris don't go to stable organizations that are slow because of caution and bureaucracy, that are intrinsically hierarchical and competitive instead of collaborative, where people hire others who are less able than they are, and punish creative failure irrespective of the reasonableness of the effort.

Management needs to also realize that traditional job security isn't a goal for Ferraris. They will stay with an organization as long as the work is really exciting, there's the potential to leave a huge footprint and maybe make a lot of money, relationships with colleagues are really good—and going to work is deeply satisfying and really fun. As long as those conditions exist, Ferraris are committed to tremendous achievement in that organization. But that may not be a commitment to that organization.

It takes enormous confidence to be a Ferrari; people don't become Ferraris until they've wrestled with growth, crashing, rebooting, and relaunching. For them, although the options of this company may never resurface, there's always another company…another idea…a different way to win. When the current endeavor goes south, they're disappointed, and perhaps angered. But they're not scared.

The stable world embraced the value of teams and

groups; at work, fairness was defined as identical treatment and outcomes for everyone, irrespective of differences in contribution. Because Ferraris are extraordinarily valuable in the borderless world, their insistence that they be treated as individuals could conceivably reinstate the value of individualism.

Individualism has a long history in American culture and the value of honoring individuality has proven to be a huge advantage in the borderless economy. Americans value individual initiative and reward individual creativity. We are resistant to traditional social classes and at least theoretically, we applaud a meritocracy.

My brother, Stephen Hardis, who recently retired as CEO of Eaton Corporation, told me:

> The *ultimate* success factor will prove to be the ability of individuals to cope with the effects of all of the external factors including continuing technological revolutions, inexorable pressure for productivity improvements and markedly greater performance expectations. The way that individuals "cope" will determine if they simply survive or whether they optimize the opportunities being created. If we consciously try and take advantage of our national characteristics by thinking in terms of the individual as *the* success factor, we will vastly improve the outcomes.

ENDNOTES

1. In 2002, young boomers are between 38 and 47, GenXers are 20 to 37, and the generation of GenD is between 15 and 30.

2. You will find two sample forms in the Appendix to help with this assessment. One asks you to evaluate what you want and the other assesses what the organization can deliver.

3. Ferguson, Charles H., "High St@akes, No Prisoners," *Times Business*, Random House, New York, 1999.

4. Petzinger, Thomas, Jr., "Talking About Tomorrow—An Interview with Kim Polese," *The Wall Street Journal*, January 1, 2000, p. R24.

5. Shell, David, "Crank It Up," *Wired*, August 2000, pp. 194–197. David Shell observes that Andreeson does not regard Netscape to be his great legacy.

6. Lardner, James, "Life Inside a Silicon Valley Start-up," *U.S. News and World Report*, December 20, 1999, p. 50.

7. Pre-IPO means before the initial public offering, or before the stock is available to the public. In the second half of the 1990s, stock prices typically soared the first day, fell over the next several days or weeks, and then continued to climb in the bull market.

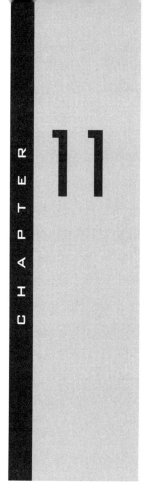

11

ORGANIZATIONS: ACHIEVE BEST FIT

- SUCCESS REQUIRES A "BEST FIT" BETWEEN AN INDIVIDUAL AND AN ORGANIZATION
- INDIVIDUALS MUST BE TRUTHFUL ABOUT WHETHER THEY'RE A FERRARI OR A FORD
- ORGANIZATIONS NEED TO PLACE GREAT WEIGHT ON A PERSON'S PERSONALITY, AMBITIONS, AND CHARACTER

The door is opened by the CEO, 34 years old, and wearing blue jeans, a T-shirt, and boots. A basketball hoop hangs on the back of the door, right next to huge plastic blow-up Crayola® crayons. People are jammed into crowded office space, most of it messy with stuff sprawled all over desks, chairs, and the floor. The hum never quits; intense conversations are going on everywhere. Suddenly there's a big bang! The CFO just knocked a hole in the wall. Welcome to the borderless start-up, where success is a work in progress and the margin between excitement and exhaustion is a thin red line.

Another door is opened by another CEO, 54 years old, and wearing a dark suit, white shirt, and Ferragamo tassel loafers. His office occupies a corner of the 34th floor where all the executive offices are clustered. As you walk the corridor to his office all you hear is silence, even though office doors are open. The CEO's office, like all those on this floor, is hung with Remingtons and other masters of the American Western art tradition. The art and the wood and the maroon leather furniture convey stability and prosperity. Tradition is clearly revered in this organization.

The CEO of the dot-com start-up would be as out of place in the 34th floor corner office as the CEO in that office would be in a start-up. To achieve success, organizations have to achieve a "best fit" between the characteristics and requirements of the organization and those of its employees.

There are major differences in the values and styles of stable organizations and borderless companies. People who prefer stable organizations value security highly, but those who prefer borderless start-ups view traditional security as limiting. Employees in stable organizations are comfortable being treated as members of a group, but borderless employees insist they be treated as individuals.

The person who is successful in a stable organization likes being a member of a large and preeminent organization and gains pride and an identity from that commitment. Although that person may poke fun at the organization's rules and procedures, that individual likes knowing where the lines are drawn. That person understands the value of precedent and tradition. That same individual would be very uncomfortable and would most likely fail in a situation that called for entrepreneurial qualities.

The key to success is achieving a best fit between the employee's values, styles, and priorities and the conditions, requirements, and payoffs that an organization offers. Where there's a best fit, employees have the personal qualities that are likely to result in their being successful within that organization.

I worked for IBM as an outsider, a lecturer and consultant, for about 25 years. When Tom Bouchard, then IBM's executive vice president for Human Resources asked me to come and work for the company and redesign their executive and management development program, I refused. "It wouldn't work, Tom," I said, "I'm okay as an outsider. But I'd be ineffective as an insider. I'm much too forthright to be accepted as an IBMer."

The wider range of organizational conditions that were created by the advent of borderless organizations means there are no "best companies" or "best practices." There's no one size that fits all. Instead, there's a best fit—a match between an individual's values, priorities, and behaviors and those of an organization.

How do organizations successfully attract, motivate, involve, and retain people? They achieve a best fit. They select people who have the personal characteristics that are likely to result in their being successful within the organization as it is or will be, and whose most important needs and desires can be met. Ideal outcomes are achieved when there is a best fit between the requirements and opportunities of the organization and the capacities and priorities of the employee.

Best fit, compatibility between what the organization requires and the employee desires, leads to high motivation, comfort, and success. Bad fit leads to discomfort, high stress, and failure. Without best fit, the chances for success and retention plummet; with best fit, the chances for success soar.

DIFFERENT KINDS OF ORGANIZATIONS

At the dawn of the 21st century, there is a much broader range of organizational characteristics, a far wider range of people's attributes, and a greater insistence on individuality than we have seen before. As a result, the tasks of management in the 21st century are much more complicated and customized than they were in the 20th century.

In the second half of the 20th century, virtually every person and every organization was fundamentally alike. Organizations were stable and employees generally satisfied their needs for a safe, predictable, and secure life. In the

21st century, management needs to pay serious attention to *individuals*. The core differences between individuals require that organizations customize many practices to engage people, especially Ferraris, and keep them satisfied and motivated.

Organizations now need to select people for management who have excellent people skills. Management must now relate to and lead many people whose views and priorities are very different from their own. Making that task more difficult is the fact that customizing responsibilities, working conditions, and rewards is a major change from organizations' historic concept of fairness. In the 20th century, fairness was defined as everyone being treated identically. When people are responded to as individuals, fairness involves different outcomes for different people, all played out on a level playing field. Avoiding jealousy and resentment, the hue and cry of "Why did she get that?!," requires managers with a deft touch who generate a lot of respect for their fairness.

Not so very long ago, there weren't major differences in the core motives of most people in the different generations and there weren't huge differences in the cultures, values, and practices of most organizations. But, today we have far greater differences in priorities between people than we ever had before.

Some people love the meteoric growth and absence of precedent and bureaucracy in a start-up, while others need the clarity that's provided by formal structure and detailed processes. The perks of bigness and deep pockets—secretaries, well-furnished large offices, imposing buildings, company planes, and cars—appeal to many people who would be very unhappy with the garage-sale furniture and cramped cubicles of a start-up.

Although some people are drawn to the pressure-cooker heroics of a borderless start-up, others find working in an organization that sees an eight-hour day as a day's work as really important. There's an enormous difference between being responsible for a whole project, which often happens in a start-up, and being one of many who contribute, which is normal in a Fortune 500 company. Many people prefer job security, dependable compensation and benefits, a slower pace, and few surprises. Lots of people still prefer tenure, implicit or contractual, to the potential of options.

Security and no nasty surprises are still enormously important to a huge number of people. Researchers at the John J. Heldrich Center for Workforce Development at Rutgers University and the Center for Research Analysis at the University of Connecticut interviewed almost 6,000 American workers between 1998 and 2000.[1] Despite the previous seven to nine years of economic good times and the extraordinarily low unemployment rate, nearly 90 percent said they were worried about job security and whether they would be able to keep their job until they retired.

Stable goals are still widely shared. It's important to

remember that many stable organizations have historically been among America's most admired places to work.

If you think of a best company as a best fit, a best company is necessarily in the eyes of the beholder. A best company does a superb job of being honest about its values and priorities and it selects people who will resonate with what it offers and succeed within its culture. Every organization has to become very insightful about its own "soft" characteristics as well as those of the people it wants to attract and keep.

Fortune magazine named The Container Store chain as the best company to work for in America in 1999 and 2000. The Container Store sells boxes, shelves, and jars...mostly it sells storage. This is not glamourous. There are no stock options. There are no sales commissions. The Web is nowhere in sight.

The Container Store people believe that succeeding is simple: Just treat people like you want to be treated. The company believes in family values and employees say they're all members of the company family. There are no secrets because management opens the books. Employees report that the company has made them better people and the stores make the world a better, more organized place. People expect to work at The Container Store for a long time. They're happy there.

The Container Store has done an unusually good job of developing and articulating the company's values and selecting people who are a great fit. A sense of family, trust and pride, long-term employment, and a slow pace of change appeal to Container Store people. And the company does a great job of selecting people who share its values and the experience it offers.

A second group of organizations, which includes the majority of large and mature businesses, has found it necessary to transform themselves over roughly the past 15 years. They are transitional companies—previously successful and now forced to change because they're unsuccessful in borderless conditions. This group includes the majority of our most famous and revered corporations: General Electric, IBM, Hewlett-Packard, and the like. Because true transformation is exceedingly rare, organizations that set out on a path of transformation generally continue on that path permanently.

The third and smallest group of organizations was founded in the past 20 years and blossomed in the 1990s. Borderless organizations range from large and successful older companies like Microsoft, Sun Microsystems, QUALCOMM, and eBay to successful Web start-ups like CBSMarketwatch.com. Borderless organizations' core business is technology itself or they could not exist without computers or the Net. A critical element they have in common is that they were created within the last 15 to 20 years when turbulent conditions already existed. Since these companies were established in borderless conditions, they take for granted ever-rising requirements for major innovation, continuous adaptability, and accelerating speed.

The differences in needs and characteristics among stable, transitional, and borderless organizations means different kinds of people will be selected to lead these different kinds of organizations (see Table 11-1). In stable organizations, for example, in which basic change isn't necessary, leaders tend to be selected on the basis of what they already know—their knowledge, skills, and experiences. In The Container Store chain, for instance, it's appropriate that leaders are required to truly believe in family values and have in-depth relevant retail experience. The Container Store's next CEO is very likely to be an insider.

Transitional organizations—ones that are in the process of trying to change in major ways and become nimble, fast, and innovative—are more likely to select an outsider or an internal maverick, like Jack Welch was in his earlier years at General Electric. New CEOs are often chosen because their personal characteristics are very different from those of the previous CEOs. Transitional organizations are well advised not to select leaders with the values and characteristics of the previous leadership because the conditions the new leaders have to create need to be markedly different from those that previously existed.

Organizations, especially start-ups, that are created when borderless conditions already exist, most need an entrepreneur who has either the necessary financial or

TABLE 11-1 Different Kinds of Organizations and the Selection of Leaders

	STABLE LARGE AND MATURE ORGANIZATION	TRANSITIONAL ORGANIZATION	BORDERLESS START-UP ORGANIZATION
Objective	Run it!	Change it!	Grow it!
Leaders Need	Operational skills	Leadership skills and confidence-building characteristics	Entrepreneurial and technical skills. As the organization grows, they need personal maturity
Environment	Political, because it's very hierarchical	Somewhat political	Apolitical
Leaders most need	Experience and deep knowledge of the business	Integrity, believability, and trustworthiness	Dedication, adaptability, commitment, focus, and passion
Major error	Select for status quo	Select a cheer-leader with no follow-through	Select for technical ability and ignore interpersonal immaturity
People style	Group processes: Everyone handled the same way	Moving from group to customized approach	Individualized and customized
Insider or outsider	An insider with immense experience	An outsider or an internal maverick	An insider at start-up, then either is possible

technical skills that are needed and the intuition that's necessary to successfully grow a very new business. Borderless organizations have little or no past to guide or impede them as they move into an uncertain future. That's a powerful asset because they don't have a culture based on conditions that no longer exist. It's also a liability in that the organization has no history or only a short track record of success. That's why the leader of a borderless organization has to be a realist who is simultaneously an optimist because that person needs to generate a convincing sense of a hopeful future for employees.

Stable and borderless organizations are very different in terms of the kinds of experiences they offer, their priorities and values, the amount of compensation people might earn, levels of risk or job security, and the opportunities they offer for creativity and leadership. While some people love unpredictability, risk, and autonomy, other people like to know their place and get their orders.

DIFFERENT KINDS OF PEOPLE

There are basically two types of organizations—stable and borderless—just as there are basically two types of people—Fords and Ferraris. Both people and organizations can be in transition from one state to the other. Just as transitional organizations try to transform themselves from stable to borderless organizations, people try to change from Fords to Ferraris. The transitional state in both people and organizations is always difficult because major transformation always involves core change.

There are significant differences in the percentage of Fords, transitional people, and Ferraris in different cohorts. A cohort is a 10-year age span (e.g., 20 to 29-year-olds). Within the age group of 50 to 59, perhaps 80 percent are Fords, 15 percent are transitional, and 5 percent are Ferraris. Among the 20 to 29-year-olds, perhaps 60 percent are Fords, 20 percent are transitional, and 20 percent are Ferraris. The percentage of people in the three groups will vary by age and industry.

Depression-impacted Fords are security seekers. Their key goal is first to achieve security, and then some reasonable level of success and a comfortable and predictable life. Although the great majority are far too young to have lived through the Depression, they learned the lesson of putting security first from their parents or grandparents. Or they saw the local factory close, putting a town out of work. Or they were let go and discovered their skills had little value. Because all security seekers are affected by the Depression and share a fear of financial disaster, people in this group are far more alike than they are individual.

Ferraris are a small but vitally important group. These people thrive on risk, change, and unpredictability because they see far more opportunity than threat in those conditions. They've lived through bad economic times as well as good and their innate optimism is tempered by a strong sense of reality. Honed by hard times during which they survived and might even have succeeded, they are genuinely confident.

Although small, this group is disproportionately important because these people are the natural leaders in borderless conditions. People who prefer turbulence and change are far more likely to succeed in borderless conditions and their success can inspire confidence and hope in an organization's Fords.

Fords prefer merry-go-rounds; Ferraris choose roller coasters. People who flourish in stable conditions are very different from those who succeed in borderless conditions.

The third group of people—the transitionals—is the most difficult cluster to understand and motivate. These people look like and talk like Ferraris, but although a few ultimately become courageous and entrepreneurial, the great majority of them never develop the requisite confidence and personal strength.

This group is made up of two subgroups: One cluster includes young people, especially fairly recent college graduates, who have no memory of the last severe recession which occurred between 1981 and 1982, and they've never seen a prolonged bear market. Growing up during two decades of good times, even after the stock market tumbled in 2000 and the economy stumbled into recession, this group continues to say they expect to achieve major success within—at the most—five years. But their confidence and optimism are illusory. Without the experience of hard times, courage and tenacity are untested and, therefore, undeveloped. We can't know what this group's longer term attitudes and expectations will be because that will largely depend on what happens in the economy during the next five years or so.

The other people in the transitional group initially chose stable careers. They joined GM, IBM, or 3M, or they became accountants or lawyers. They moved to borderless companies, especially start-ups, or they became day traders in the second half of the 1990s, either because the potential rewards were so breathtaking or because their self-esteem required that they join start-ups to assure themselves that they, too, had what it took to be Ferraris.

When the dot-coms crashed and the stock market tanked in 2000, the great majority of these people went back to the kinds of organizations and careers they had originally selected before the buoyant good times started. Many of these people took a double blow: They were financially burned and they learned they weren't Ferraris after all. Most of these people learned they were Ferrari-wannabes.

The transitional group includes people who want to be Ferraris and aren't; young people who are still in the process of developing strengths and confidence, and a very small number of Fords who discovered that borderless conditions can be exhilarating.

AFTER APRIL 2000

In the second half of the 1990s, especially, the goal of making money, lots and lots of money, eclipsed other choices for many Americans, most of them in their 20s and 30s. Many people made career decisions on the basis of the possibility of acquiring big money. Affluent youth in the nation's best universities disdained the professions and consulting to join Wall Street or they made it to Silicon Valley or Silicon Alley. For the first time in the history of the world, America produced a large class of affluent people.

But that changed: April 2000 marked the start of a bear market, the end of the IPO market, and the beginning of the dot-com decline. Some dot-comers, especially those in their early 20s, became angry, confused, and bitter. For the first time in their lives, their ebullient optimism gave way to fear. While the specific fear is not having a job, the underlying anxiety is, "What's going on? I'm supposed to be a millionaire by now! Am I too late? Is it over?"

The Web was viewed as a major technological breakthrough for delivering information and products, for communicating, and for selling. With a technology that new, no one knew either the limitations or the possibilities, so many business models were tried. People were placing huge bets on best guesses. As the guesses were rewarded with fortunes, even vast sums of red ink were interpreted as assets. Many organizations were created just to be flipped so the early insiders could take the money and run. The Web was an inconceivable, glorious money machine, until investors started asking for profits, of which there were very few. The NASDAQ stock market, which specializes in technology companies, lost half of its value in six months. After April, caution began to replace euphoria.

The possibility of proving to themselves that they, too, had the right stuff and could end up with lots of money attracted people who were not intrinsically confident and optimistic. The opportunity to perceive yourself as a Ferrari rather than a Ford, and the availability of transformational amounts of money, made for a lot of bad fit.

It is a bad fit between an employee and an organization when people join borderless companies because the psychological and financial payoffs are immensely seductive, but, at heart, they're Fords. Fords aren't confident enough to deal with the chaotic and extremely demanding 24/7 conditions that are normal in a borderless organization, especially a start-up.

Will a less ebullient economy change the financial expectations and goals of people who chose to join borderless start-ups? Pragmatically, that depends partially on the length and severity of a downturn. It also depends on people's personal history and the outcome of their experiences.

People's priorities, goals, and values take years to formulate and they don't change in the course of a year or two. Even after April 2000, many knowledge workers in their 20s and just out of school continued to have the highest expectations, reflecting the fact that all they've really known is a heady economy and a soaring market. In a survey done in February 2001, college students remained incredibly optimistic.[2] They expected immediate success in terms of promotions and compensation. While 81 percent thought it would take them 10 years or less to achieve their career goals, 48 percent thought it would take 5 years or less. One student said, "While it is true that it takes time to succeed, I think that 2 to 5 years should be enough."

With little or no prior work or recession experience, most in this group are likely to become disenchanted with the dream of glamour and quick riches if the great times don't return. Their lack of experience with the normal cycles of the economy is likely to lead most of them to exaggerate the short-term negatives and ignore the long-term positives. These young people haven't had enough experience coping with harder times to develop the skills to do it or the confidence that they could. Especially as they move into marriage and become parents, reasonable economic security will become more attractive to many of them than a risky ride to possible riches.

The real Ferraris are people for whom high risk and fast change are vastly more preferable than security and predictability. These people are risk creators and when they achieve success, they do something that is incomprehensible to people with less self-confidence: They leave the arena in which they've succeeded and begin to do something else.

The youngest of this group are in their mid-30s, veterans of the major layoffs of the 1980s and early 1990s. Confident, they may leave the battle-scarred turf of dot-coms only to move into the next sector that promises a shot at moving the needle and huge payoffs. These people are so confident and optimistic that they really are different from everyone else.

Good fit, which is at the heart of employee satisfaction and organizational success, requires that people and organizations really know what they're like and what they want to become at a level of honesty that may require considerable courage. Eaton Corporation, a pillar of Cleveland's economy for more than a century, had to look squarely at its traditional product line and its century-old culture, and decide what to keep and what to jettison in the new borderless conditions. Looking in the mirror unflinchingly may be hard to do if your present qualities and characteristics are not those that are now most useful and in vogue. But honesty is the only way to get a best fit.

- Organizations must select people whose core needs or highest priorities can be met.

- Organizations must select people whose attitudes and behaviors are compatible with those of the present or future organization.

- Organizations must select people whose expectations can be met.

- In turn, individuals have to know what most matters to them at this time, and the conditions in which they're most likely to flourish.

Realistically, the best fit will keep evolving as people's needs and priorities reflect what's happening in the economy as well as their personal development. Best fit is a moving target in a dynamic economy.

ENDNOTES

1. Van Horn, Carl E., "New Economy Not Helping Gore," *USA Today*, July 17, 2000, p. 17A.

2. "Bulls on the Campus" *San Diego Union-Tribune*, February 19, 2001, p. C1.

12 ORGANIZATIONS: MANAGE TECHNOLOGY'S OUTCOMES

- KEEP IT SIMPLE; KEEP IT FOCUSED
- CREATE NEW RULES OF ETIQUETTE
- GET THE PEOPLE PART RIGHT

M easurement is a tool; it shouldn't be an occupation. Jeffrey Pfeiffer of the Stanford Graduate School of Business, met a woman who worked for a large oil company.[1] She told him that she was responsible for the 105 measures the company took. When Pfeiffer asked how many of the measures she paid attention to, the woman said "None."

People in that oil company measured everything they could think of because: (1) no one could accuse them of omitting something important; (2) inclusiveness, "making my list longer than yours," was a competitive ploy; and (3) taking measurements was so easy. Because too many measurements make the data unmanageable and incomprehensible, 105 measures actually equated to none.

IT can create an explosion of new data, make the instant dissemination of information possible, and allow us to take complex measures of everything. That can be really expensive and a really dumb thing to do.

Data are bits of information, facts, and factoids. In music terms, data are the musical notes.

Information is data that have been organized in such a way that they answer a question. Information is the equivalent of the musical score.

Knowledge is information that has been analyzed and conceptualized. Knowledge is the artist's interpretation of the musical score.

Because IT makes it amazingly easy to amass huge amounts of data, the forest is usually too filled with trees to see very much. Too often, getting the data is assumed to be the end point. I recently received the projected budget for the year 2002 for a company I work with. The budget book is 114 pages long and it is filled with computer-generated columns, bar charts, and graphs. What really matters in the new budget? I don't know: So many data are presented that it's not possible to see anything.

Compiling useless data is frustrating; drowning in a sea of irrelevant data is exhausting. That's why the imperative questions (or hypotheses) always have to be about what's most important for the business of the business to know. Information and knowledge are the result of answering the right questions—as directly, clearly, and simply as possible.

Getting the data is only the first step and it is never the final goal. The essential task is to transform data into something understandable and useful, into information that can then become knowledge.

The most critical part of creating value from data is understanding the business model of the organization, because that's key to knowing what the institution really needs to know. A stable manufacturing company, for example, might focus on keeping costs low by reducing errors in its manufacturing process through systematic quality improvements. That company would want to monitor the reduction in flawed products, for example, or the increase in running time for its production machines. In contrast, a borderless Web-based retail company would want their Web site to be very attractive and user-friendly. That company would want to know if changes in the Web site resulted in a higher or lower percentage of customers who clicked on, stayed on, and completed a transaction.

Getting valuable information and knowledge from raw data depends on identifying the really significant and productive questions that the business needs to have answered. The largest error is starting an analysis without the pivotal questions. The next worst mistake is to frame the questions or take measurements in terms of what IT can handle instead of in terms of what really matters. That's what the oil company in the beginning of this chapter did.

The best use of IT does not come from a sophisticated understanding of IT. It comes, instead, from really understanding the needs and priorities of the business of the business. The best use of IT and the best measurements come from knowing what's most important to the business at this point in time.

In fact, IT's mechanistic systems can create major problems, as we saw in the example of Coast Pharmaceutical in Chapter 8, "Information Technology Is Not Emotionally Neutral." Larry Ellison, founder and chairman of Oracle, has observed that computing erred in the 1990s when the industry ran applications on the client/server system because the industry focused on automating processes instead of getting key information to decision makers.[2] The result was distributed complexity and fragmented data instead of relevant answers to business' key questions.

Having large amounts of cheaper and faster data does not automatically improve information, the organization's competitive position, or the profitability of the enterprise. Without an understanding of the organization, its core business, and the priorities and needs of its members, IT does not solve fundamental problems.

Organizations can't afford to fall in love with technology for its own sake. It's important that deengineering—keeping things simple—followed reengineering. In deengineering, for instance, instead of developing complex software that differentiates between casual and key customers, important customers are given a special phone number or fax number to call, or email address to use.

Technology has to be held to rigorous criteria: It must advance the business more effectively than other ways of doing things and it must make work more interesting or working conditions more responsive to people's needs. Any other outcomes are expensive mistakes.

NEW RULES OF ETIQUETTE

I have a new hero. On August 10, 2000, I sent an email to John A. Zondlo of the Los Alamos National Laboratory. The automatic reply I received said:

> Subject: Away From My Mail
> I will not be reading my mail until Aug. 15, 2000.
> Your mail regarding "..." will be read when I return.

Does every email need or deserve an immediate reply? Can't some emails rest a while in an electronic inbox so they kind of answer themselves? Which emails can be ignored? Are people supposed to answer emails when they're on vacation? What are the rules about email...and snail mail, phone calls, and faxes...in your organization?

Because technology creates accessibility, and the Web

demands speed, and layoffs reduce the number of people doing the work but rarely the amount of work, an awful lot of people are working much longer and harder than they used to, but that's not even enough to let them stay in place. Since most people have a job at work that keeps expanding and another at home, overload is widespread and it's exhausting. Overload creates stress and rising performance requirements create anxiety: "Am I doing enough to please my boss so I'm not the first one laid off?"

Management needs to become very clear about what it expects from employees in terms of hours, output, and accessibility. Reducing the stress of overload requires a best fit between the employee's and the organization's ideas about what a normal work week is and how accessible people are expected to be. Choices need to be made between the competing goals of being on duty every hour of every day, and having the right, except in crises, of ignoring work during what is accepted as private time.

- Are you expected to supply contact information when you're out of town?
- Is it okay to ignore email and not carry a pager when on vacation?
- Are emails supposed to be read and answered the day they arrive?
- Are you supposed to send reports and attachments to everyone who might be interested or are you sup-

posed to make sure the material is relevant to every recipient?

- Should every report have a one-page summary with an email address where the recipient can access the full analysis?

...and so on.

Some organizations demand more and some people love the phone calls and crazy hours, the dizzying speed, and the ever-rising requirements of 24/7 in a borderless start-up. For other people, less intrusion because of the stress it creates and more private time that is really private have become precious.

There's a wide range of opinions on this subject, so organizations and employees need to make their needs, priorities, and expectations extremely clear. Organizations must decide how employee-friendly and flexible they're willing to be. People need to have an honest dialogue with themselves, their family, and their organizations about the boundaries to their accessibility that they need. Employees have to decide what's most important to them and evaluate whether or not their current choices foster those outcomes. Employees and their organizations need to know if there's a best fit or if changes in work or life choices are necessary.

There is no single "right" set of expectations and rules. Different organizations end up with different rules because their circumstances are different and, therefore, so are their expectations about what people should do and what behaviors make an employee excellent. An organization's rules are based on assumptions and those assumptions reflect the organization's priorities and values.

Some of the assumptions and values that need to be explored, debated, and made very clear are:

- Exhaustion is a counterproductive "remedy" for a lack of time.
- Creating limits on work is a shared responsibility of employees and their employers.
- Organizations that are in strident competition have a right to call on employees at any time.
- Flexibility over when and where work is done is desirable.
- It's necessary to work at eliminating as many superfluous work activities as possible.
- It's better to keep people's private lives, including child care, out of the workplace.
- Many people have major responsibilities to parents and children and for their sake as well as the others, they need to meet them.
- A borderless economy calls for permanent 24/7 accessibility. There is no such thing as private time and places.
- Organizations need to respect people's personal lives because people need human connections and personal time.

- Downtime, without any work, fosters creativity and performance.

We need a new etiquette. Organizations have to be very clear about whether or not there are some parameters that define how many hours of work are expected or whether employees are expected to continue working until the work is finished, irrespective of how long that takes. Organizations need to be very clear about whether or not employees have real private time and space, and, if so, when and what kinds of intrusions in private time are okay and which cross the line. People need to know what expectations an organization has in order to know whether or not those rules would work for them.

GET THE PEOPLE PART RIGHT

Getting the people part right isn't about being nice. When the focus is solely on technology and human needs are ignored, the outcome is bad business results.

A wonderful example of bad practices is the usual design of technology-based customer call centers. An effective call center delivers outstanding service and employees remain with the company and at the call center for years. Ineffective call centers deliver poor levels of service and their turnover is very high and expensive. Effective and ineffective call centers use the same technology. Why, then, are some successful but the majority are not?[3]

The employees of high-performance call centers feel fulfilled by their jobs. These employees do more than just answer the phone: They change tasks and keep learning, they're often members of problem-solving teams, and their jobs are designed to make their work satisfying and rewarding.

USAA is a very successful American insurance company which is rated very highly by its customers who typically stay with the company forever. USAA has the highest rates of customer and employee retention in the industry. Their call center employees are enthusiastic about their jobs: They get twice the average amount of training that's typical in the insurance business and they are encouraged to think—to inform a divisional problem-solving team, for example, about customer needs that could be met by improving service.

The jobs at unsuccessful call centers are stressful and unfulfilling. Employees have little or no opportunity to do anything other than answer phones, usually on a tight and measured time schedule. The work is narrow, soon mastered, and very repetitive. These employees don't have opportunities to learn or to contribute to changes they think would improve service. Not surprisingly, they usually feel isolated and under immense pressure. It's no wonder that, over time, the service levels of these employees decline, and then the employees quit.

The work environment, people's jobs, the work they do,

and the processes people use in their work all need to be designed so that people are motivated to do the work and do it well. People stay because they feel productive, included, and significant.

People issues are particularly difficult and important in today's virtual organizations. Because IT enables people to communicate inexpensively and in real time all over the world, many organizations are taking advantage of the flexibility that that creates. Increasingly, organizations are made up of both permanent members and temporary employees. For instance, I'm on the Human Resources Advisory Board of The Concours Group, a consulting and research organization that specializes in IT-related issues. It is cutting-edge both in the content of the work it does and in its structure. Created approximately five years ago, it has roughly 70 permanent members ranging from office assistants to PhDs who live and work in North America and Europe. Concours is both a real and a virtual organization as it continuously puts together changing combinations of permanent members and temporary employees with specialized knowledge to work on consulting or research projects.

IT makes fluid partnering, quickly and easily creating new combinations of organizations and people, possible. Concours is successful in using teams with ever-changing members because the company understands that fluid partnering requires a more horizontal structure of peers than the traditional hierarchical structure. On Concours projects leaders do far more listening and encouraging than ordering and judging.

Concours also realizes that selecting people who are mature, confident self-starters is critical because both permanent members and temporary team employees have to be comfortable working without traditional support and feedback from bosses, and they may need to be able to work alone as well as with strangers. And lastly, Concours has found that the enabling qualities of personality and character are decisively important because alignment and commitment in changing relationships come from trust, shared values, and shared priorities.

Cisco Corporation successfully integrated more than 50 acquisitions between 1993 and 2000.[4] The company is famous for creating powerful alliances with the organizations it acquires. Cisco is able to do that because the company pays a lot of attention to the "hard" variables of finance and technology and to the "soft" variables of chemistry and culture. Before acquiring a company, Cisco asks if there's a "good fit" between its leaders and those of the organization they're thinking of acquiring. What is the other company's management style and is it compatible with ours? What are the basic values of the other organization and are they a good fit with ours?

If the technology, customer base, finances, and strategy are a good fit, but the chemistry, compatibility, and values are not, Cisco doesn't merge with or acquire that company. Cisco is one of very few organizations that handle mergers and acquisitions really well, because Cisco never forgets that although technology makes it easy to blend organizations, it's the people factors that determine whether the combination will be a success or a failure. Perhaps most telling of all, although technically Cisco acquires other companies, psychologically they create partnerships with the other organizations. That's why Cisco is so good at it.

It is ironic but logical that in a technology-dominated world the personal or human moments become more important. In all the project teams I've worked on, with email, phones, and faxes making communication pretty easy, still, that generally isn't enough. Although there are people who are much more comfortable "meeting" on computer screens rather than face-to-face, in my personal experience, everyone is dying to meet. People want to get together, talk, and see people's faces; they want to get the feel, the measure of everyone else.

People want to see especially those people they don't know and have never met. The reason is very simple: We look at people's faces, we scan their eyes and mouth, we look for the grin that says the harsh words were a joke, we're sensitive to body language—to finger tapping or a glance at a watch—we listen to tones…most of the data we use to interpret a communication is not in the words. Especially when we're communicating with strangers, the fewer nonverbal cues we have, the greater the chance we won't get it; we'll misinterpret what was said.

The most effective communication is still face-to-face. E-communication is invaluable and vulnerable; that's why people need to get together and chat, discuss, debate—and eat. Then they can have what psychiatrist Edward Hallowell calls a "human moment."[5] The human moment occurs when people are in the same place, they're genuinely focused on each other, and they give out and they receive messages that really communicate and are emotionally clear. That's when people really "hear" each other.

The human moment is about connecting, the feeling you and the other person are in synch: You're hearing them and they're hearing you and you're both bouncing off each other's ideas and observations. When we communicate electronically, the context, the inferences, and the "Aha!" or "That's right!" that we get in the human moment are missing. In our wired, distanced, and airborne lives, connecting is becoming more and more rare.

Effective organizations make sure that their people have opportunities to meet and connect; ineffective organizations don't. Organizations that ignore people's basic human needs for human moments are far less effective than they could be because trust, which is critical for communicating and collaborating, is the outcome of connecting.

Meeting human needs is vastly more critical and difficult in IT-impacted conditions than it is in traditional organizations. It's simply harder for people to feel significant, connected, and appreciated in a virtual or blended organization that includes people with different values and ways of doing things, when there are few face-to-face meetings and people and organizations have no shared history and little in common. Effective organizations keep that in mind and manage to satisfy people's basic human needs.

Organizations need to control how they use technology and not let the potentials of the technology control them. That involves keeping things as simple as possible and focused on the business' critical issues. Because technology can make people accessible and available 24/7, organizations need to examine the assumptions they make about people's availability. From that examination, they need to formulate the rules of behavior and the accepted etiquette in that organization.

In those organizations where there are few human moments, especially, management needs to have a strong commitment to creating those conditions that will help people to satisfy their core needs. In other words, organizations need to spend the money so people can meet and eat—and they need to expend the energy so people feel purposeful, included, and appreciated.

Endnotes

1. Webber, Alan M., "Why Can't We Get Anything Done?", *Fast Company*, June 2000, pp. 169–180.

2. "The Net Imperative," *The Economist*, June 26, 1999, p. 56.

3. Dave Ulrich and I were involved in a Concours Group Re.sults® Project that investigated these and related issues. Birge, Eileen, and the Concours Group, *HR: Human Resources Management in a Technology-Driven Environment*, 1999.

4. Thurm, Scott, "Joining the Fold," *The Wall Street Journal,* March 1, 2000, pp. A1, A12.

5. Hallowell, Edward M., "The Human Moment at Work," *Harvard Business Review*, January–February 1999, pp. 58–66.

13

ORGANIZATIONS: DON'T LEAP INTO MAJOR CHANGE

- CHANGE EFFORTS MUST DO NO HARM
- ORGANIZATIONS MUST AVOID FAILURE; IT INVITES MORE
- SUCCESS MUST BE DESIGNED INTO EVERY CHANGE EFFORT

In the early 1990s, my colleagues Norm Schoenfeld and Pat Curran and I spent a lot of time at one of the seven Baby Bells, the regional phone companies that had been spun off from AT&T. All of the Bells, including Ma Bell, had become aware that they were the epitome of a stable organization and, as a result, they were hugely unprepared for competition. Our task, which we accomplished, was to do an analysis of the strengths and weaknesses of the various parts of the company and make specific recommendations for improvement. We interviewed about 100 people, read all the in-house material including financial statements and business plans, sat in on many meetings, and generally observed what was going on over the course of several months.

The Bells were and are very large companies with enormous revenues, a huge number of customers—and a 100-year-old culture that grew out of a monopoly. It would be hard to imagine an organization that could be less prepared for the Darwinism of borderless competition than the Bell companies.

Change—major core change—was clearly called for. The CEO proposed the simultaneous restructuring of the company from hundreds of customer centers to less than 20; the reengineering of many of their important processes; and the installation of a major quality improvement program. Although there was agreement among the officers, executives, middle management, professionals, union bosses, and blue-collar employees about the need for major change, there was heated disagreement over the timing of the changes.

The proposed changes were going to cause an enormous disruption in people's lives. It was estimated that over 80 percent of employees would have to move just because of the consolidation of the customer centers. That meant their spouses or partners would probably have to find new jobs, they'd have to sell their homes and buy new ones, and their children would have to go to new schools.

The disruption at work would be just as great. The complexity of the proposed reengineering and quality improvement processes was clear to see because maps of the existing processes and the probable changes were posted in diagrams that encircled large rooms and spilled out into the long corridors.

The goal was to change everything, and there was pretty strong agreement that that was the way to go. The only question was whether to do it all at once and get it over with—whether it would be wiser to go slowly, create small pilot programs, test them, and roll the successful programs out gradually. The corporation was split between those who claimed it was kinder to rip the bandage off fast and those who insisted that it was wiser to avoid unnecessary disruptions to employees and their families, and catastrophic mistakes at work. If that more cautious and prudent course were to be followed, it would be necessary to take the time to learn what worked and what didn't, and therefore change would be implemented gradually.

Morale was already terrible when we arrived and it grew decisively worse during the months we were there. The company had had massive downsizings and people were expecting more. Customers and government regulators were angered by a huge deterioration in service, and accusations that the company was failing to meet its responsibilities made headlines in all the regional newspapers. Anxiety and fear always give birth to rumors, and rumors were multiplying about huge changes that were definitely coming, but no one could say what they involved or what the time frame would be. People's moods were spiraling downward as they felt anxious, scared, uncertain, and depressed, as well as resentful. Not surprisingly, there was a loss of confidence in the leadership. It wasn't a good time to try and rally the troops.

The CEO decided to take the fast path and rip the bandage off. All kinds of changes were instituted immediately. The result was chaos. We never did get a chance to implement our recommendations. When we returned to that company's headquarters about two years later, all but one of the officers that we had known had been replaced by new people.

There is a credo in medicine that applies perfectly to the issue of core change: First, do no harm. A change process must not contribute to the despair of failure or the agony of anxiety. No major change effort should be undertaken until and unless the probability of success is much higher than that of failure. Failure has to be avoided; failure demotivates and repetitive failure demoralizes.

The discipline of requiring success in a major change effort was rarely applied from the mid-1980s to the mid-1990s, especially, when all kinds of organizations in every kind of industry set out to achieve a massive and fundamental transformation. The goal of transformation was embraced by executives who had become aware that the world had been transformed; the world had become border-less and a borderless world required far greater speed, deci-siveness, and innovation than organizations had ever need-ed before. The result was widespread acceptance of the premise that megachange was always called for. Organizations that really needed core transformation and businesses that only needed a little tweaking, all set out to achieve core change as fast as possible.

The idea that a series of small and effective sequential innovations could amount to large change was generally dismissed as too cautious and old-fashioned. That view was spearheaded by the gurus and practitioners of the Quality Movement like Edward Deming and Reengineering's Jim Champy and Mike Hammer, views which were then in their heyday.[1] Both the Quality and Reengineering Movements were grounded in engineering and statistics and they ignored the impact on people of the huge systemic changes, both positive and negative, that they either set out to achieve or that accidentally happened.

Major change programs are usually introduced with great fanfare. While there's often some lip service about the difficulties of the journey, most of the communication is really the call: "Troops! Into the future!" It's very rare for executives to acknowledge that major change is hard to achieve and always takes an uneven and uncertain path because there are always significant and unexpected out-comes that no one can predict. It's very unusual for executives to be up front and say that massive, basic change efforts are rarely successful in their entirety, and many actually fail to achieve any significant progress.

The normal cheerleading by management encourages people to get on the bandwagon, but it also leaves people unprepared for the lack of significant success of a change effort or for the endless succession of new change efforts which usually and swiftly follow the ones that failed to make a difference. When a series of change efforts fail, the change process itself has no credibility and few champions. That's future ground for further failure.

Unless there's a brutal crisis, core change is very difficult to accomplish. A major transformation in how an organization operates or in what its people believe normally takes years. I remember when, in the late 1980s, IBM set out to improve the efficiency of its manufacturing processes and the decision was made to reduce the redundant number of quality checks that IBM made on its products. Not long after that decision was implemented, the company's internal surveys found employees accusing the corporation of unethical practices. Since ethical behavior was a keystone in the corporation's culture and practices, that finding was a shock. Further analysis revealed that a significant number of IBMers believed an appropriate—but reduced—number of quality checks cheated the customer and that, for them, was a terrible breach of ethics. It took a long time for that view to moderate.

Although change can occur faster if there's an obvious real crisis, the evolution of core change in people and organizations usually takes between three and five years. That, and the fact that basic change normally generates resistance or "push-back," is why achieving transformational change normally requires a multiyear commitment to follow through. It is very common for change programs to make their biggest investment in the kickoff of the program and the initial phases of training. After that, the level of energy and commitment exhibited by the leadership usually dissipates. That contributes to the program's failure.

Another reason for the lack of success of many efforts to create basic change in stable organizations, for example, to make them performance driven is because change efforts usually start by first trying to change the organization's culture. Although that idea sounds perfectly plausible, it is also wrong. An organization's "culture" is the sum of its expectations, attitudes, values, and normal behaviors. Those are peripheral to the core business and, as such, have no clout. Becoming team-based, for example, is a much weaker goal than earning a dollar per share. An effective change process must address what really matters; the change process has to focus its efforts on improving the performance of the business.

Looking back, it seems very clear now that the proposition of bold, major, massive change was accepted by executives in the 1980s and early 1990s because the executives knew they were floundering in the face of the new borderless reality. Their personal uncertainty seemed to justify the goal of organizational transformation to something entirely different from what the organization was actually like. The appearance of specific recipes for core change like those of reengineering and Quality provided relief for executives from their own anxiety and, for that reason, they were embraced by corporate leaders.

Megachange sounded heroic and modern, in contrast to incremental change, which was timid and wishy-washy. So, core transformation became chic. But, few leaders thought much about the effect of imposing more core changes on their people, most of whom were already traumatized by the end of job security. With a goal of massive transformation, most change efforts were not designed to achieve stages of success which would have reinforced the process and raised people's hopes, commitment, and engagement. In fact, controlled, incremental change in which stages of success were an integral part of the design would have been far more effective, most of the time.

In the case of the Baby Bell which started this chapter, for example, it would probably have had a successful experience rather than the chaos and failure that resulted from trying to do everything at once, if the company had developed a sequence of change. They needed to start by carefully experimenting with restructuring its customer centers, and reengineering for aspects of quality, in one region of its territory before requiring restructuring and reengineering throughout its region.

THE RULES OF CHANGE

Broad change, like changing an organization's culture is very hard to achieve because culture is vast and amorphous and, therefore, hard to teach or measure. The more specific the goal and the more limited the number of goals at any one time, the higher the likelihood of success, especially if there's powerful follow-through.

A change process that sets out to improve the performance of the business can, however, also change the organization's culture. That happens when the organization's decision makers are themselves models of the values, attitudes, and behaviors that the organization has now identified as what it really wants. That transformation occurs when people understand what's expected of them and how they should behave because they're working with and for people who tend to naturally do what's now considered the right things in the right way. Jack Welch, the former CEO of General Electric, who led the transformation of the corporation, would be an example of walking the talk, or the power of natural modeling.

After years of participating in change efforts, I've come up with some rules and guidelines for a successful major change effort:

- Manage to success and avoid failure. No major change effort should be initiated unless it has a good chance of succeeding.
- The organization's leaders must be models of the values, attitudes, and behaviors that are now considered most desirable.
- Goals need to be based on improving the performance of the business and not on changing the organization's culture.
- A change effort needs to be proportionate to the size of the problem and the extent of a crisis. An obvious crisis gives credibility to leaders' calls for core change.
- Change efforts should be as small, as nondisruptive, and as specific as possible.
- Plans for change must be as simple and focused as possible.
- All of management must be visibly on board.
- Management should be upbeat about the outcome of change, while they are also forthright about the likely difficulties that will be involved.
- There must be a commitment to a three- to five-year follow-through.
- Measurements should be limited to outcomes that really matter.

An organization's leaders need to be realistic as well as optimistic about how much and what kinds of changes are likely to be achieved. Stable companies, which are normally driven primarily by rules, precedent, and relationships, can certainly become performance-driven meritocracies in which output is far more important than seniority or connections, and their management can definitely learn to empower appropriately and everyone can learn to collaborate and be team players. But large, mature, stable companies don't become entrepreneurial start-ups. Although elephants can learn to dance, they never become gazelles.

BUILD SUCCESS INTO THE CHANGE PROCESS

In September 2001, I was a participant in Standard Register Corporation's meeting, Strategy Forum II. There were about 125 people in the audience, made up of the top management from across all business units and functions of the company. The purpose of the meeting was for the corporate executives, most of whom were new, to share the new direction for the company's future after nearly a year of successful restructuring and reorganization.

Standard Register is an old, stable company whose major business had been designing and producing business forms and labels. In the old days before technology and the Web changed things, a customized form could be used for many years. By the late 1990s, it was clear that this was no longer true. The drivers of change were Hewlett-Packard and Canon...software and computer innovators that continuously improved the technology. In the borderless world, many of Standard Register's traditional products could now become obsolete in a relatively short time.

In 1998, Standard Register's profits started a consistent decline. In 2000, the corporation's board appointed a new CEO, Dennis Rediker, a man who had been on the board but whose views of the business were fundamentally different from those of the incumbent CEO. Rediker and a small team of executives spent half a year exploring the root causes of the decline in corporate profits and they designed the basic strategies that would be needed to restructure the company and establish a new strategy for success in the future.

Historically, most of Standard Register's leaders had come out of sales and a salesman's goal is to increase the volume of sales. Rediker's background was in engineering, not sales, and with that different perspective, his team made the critical distinction between sales volume and profitability. The results of that analysis were very clear: Standard Register had continued to chase volume although profits were decreasing. The first step in the transformation strategy had to reverse this trend. That decision led to the closing of some manufacturing plants and to further downsizing of employees because the company was exiting unprofitable businesses as well as slashing costs.

The key strategic decision was to abandon the "revenue at any cost" business model and shift to a profit-driven business model. This meant that innovative products and services would be developed for specific market segments and customers. Because these customers would benefit from the added value, they'd be willing to pay for it. Profit and not sales volume was now the corporation's goal.

Rediker's team also concluded that the corporation needed to become far more flexible, fast, and responsive than it was and that called for a new organizational structure. Standard Register was reorganized from functional areas like manufacturing or sales into four fairly autonomous strategic business units, each with the responsibility and capability of developing its own strategies and products.

From the inception of the plan for change, the September 2001 meeting was set as the date when all layoffs and plant closings were to have been completed and the new organization structure would be in place. That was achieved. Now Dennis Rediker, the new CEO, and other executive leaders, could honestly say:

> We achieved the first phase of our change program. The closings and layoffs have been accomplished. The new business unit structure is in place with new leaders. The past is behind us. The main purpose of this meeting is to move to the next phase. Every part of every unit will decide at this meeting how it will push our corporate goals forward.
>
> Our new businesses will emphasize intellectual capital—we want new ideas for new products and services. In the new version of our company the largest investments will be in people and not machines. The goal of the restructuring was

to improve profitability. The target was set at 45 cents earnings per share for the fourth quarter of 2001. If we reach that goal, there will be bonuses. We'll come out of all this smaller, smarter, and more profitable! We are now moving positively, creating a better future than we could ever have had without these changes.

Dennis Rediker and his team created a model change process; it addressed what was most important, it remained focused and direct, its goals were achievable, and its success was visible. Because the early phase of the change process met its goals, despite the underlying anxiety that is always there when circumstances require fundamental change, employees began to trust the new executive team and feel hopeful about their future. Core change achieved through incremental success has enabled Standard Register to begin to leave its past and to move forward, creating the future of its business.

In my experience, the change processes of the 1980s and 1990s became very elaborate, ambitious, and inclusive. That's unfortunate because the simpler and more manageable things are, the more likely they are to succeed. In the next chapter, I present a generic, simple, direct, and very focused change process. I hope it leads to more frequent success in change efforts.

ENDNOTE

1. The quality movement had become very important as the widely heralded Baldrige competition became a powerful tool to get organizations to achieve core change through quality improvements. At the same time, books like Champy, James, and Hammer, Michael, *Reengineering the Corporation*, HarperCollins, New York, 1993, became best sellers and so did their workshops.

14

ORGANIZATIONS: THE CHANGE PROCESS

- A CHANGE PROCESS SHOULD BE LIMITED TO ONE PAGE
- GOALS SHOULD BE CONCRETE AND SPECIFIC
- ORGANIZATIONS MUST REWARD THE ANGELS AND FIRE THE SNAKES

In June of 1998, I spent the day with key executives of Public Service Electric and Gas, a major utility with headquarters in Newark, New Jersey. American utilities had come to the realization that because their operations and values had developed when they were monopolies, they were unprepared to compete successfully when the industry was deregulated and became competitive. Late in the afternoon the wonderful, lively discussion we were having about what Public Service needed to change was interrupted by an executive who said, "Judy, this is all very interesting. But what I need to know is how to do it. What's the first step and the second…and then the next?"

What a wonderful question I thought. The plan better be extremely focused, short, and simple because the people stuff of ambition, fear, resentment, and resistance always makes everything complicated. Simple succeeds much more often than complicated. Let's try for a plan that fits on a single page. Here, then, is my answer to the question, "Just what do we do?"

THE STEPS OF CHANGE

1. Speak the unspeakable. Step up to the real major problems.
2. Identify the business of the business, the strategy to win, and specific organizationwide goals and their due dates.
3. Be extraordinarily clear about the organization's values and the behaviors that flow from them.
4. Communicate the reasons for basic change, the hurdles to be faced, and the objectives of the business transformation.
5. Create a line-of-sight from the organizationwide business goals to individual and unit performance targets with due dates.
6. Identify thrivers, survivors, and strugglers. Select thrivers for decision-making roles.

7. Fire trouble-making strugglers.

8. Fire chronic nonperformers.

9. Start again: Reassess business and people goals and issues.

This is a simple, direct, and focused process which asks, "Where are we and what impedes our ability to succeed? What do we need to do? Who are our potential leaders and who are the individuals who must change their attitudes and behaviors or be gotten rid of?" In its broad strokes, the process is as applicable to individuals as it is to organizations.

This change process is based on the idea that first, achieving core organizational change requires the achievement of significant targets in the business of the business and not of anything peripheral to that. Second, core change requires that leaders are people who are both in favor of basic change and who are, themselves models of the values, attitudes, and behaviors that have been designated as ideal.

Although it can be desirable to involve all levels of a large organization in the development of a change program, ultimately, it's top management's responsibility to do the analytic groundwork in preparation for a change program (i.e., steps 1, 2, and 3 in the change process). Then, top management must start communicating the reasons for and the nature of the changes and that communication has to cascade down throughout the organization (i.e., step 4). The next four steps (5–8), largely involve middle management but they can impact anyone. The final step starts the process all over again. In a fast-paced world, problems and their solutions are always changing.

1. **Speak the unspeakable.** Identifying the real barriers to success takes getting down and dirty; it requires speaking the unspeakable. Speaking the unspeakable takes tremendous courage because it's a criticism of past decisions and present practices and many of the current leaders were often involved in those decisions. But if the leadership doesn't speak out about the real barriers to success, which are usually already well known to everyone in the organization, the key problems can't be addressed, leaders and the change program lack credibility, and effective change becomes very unlikely.

2. **Identify the business of the business and the strategy to win.** Change happens slowly in stable conditions. Businesses start in one industry and might continue in that business for decades, a century, or more. In contrast, in the borderless economy, whole industries expand or contract swiftly and, therefore, so do competitive advantages or niches. As a result, businesses have to ask themselves the most basic questions again and again, even several times a year: What is the business of this business? Who are our customers? Who are our competitors? What's

our strategy? What are the most important organizationwide goals for the next 6 to 12 months? What can we offer that makes us the preferred supplier?

3. **Be very clear about values.** I once saw the following posted on a fence and I wrote it down:

- Honor
- Courage
- Commitment

Without a word of explanation, I often show this list of values to a group with whom I'm meeting and I ask, "Who is this?" At least 99 percent of the time, someone calls out, "The Marines." Right. The fence I saw was at Camp Pendleton Marine Base. It is truly remarkable that all kinds of people immediately associate honor, courage, and commitment with the U.S. Marines. Values say, "This is what we are: This is what we stand for." In the midst of major change when there's uncertainty and confusion about what the right things to do are and how to do them, values provide clear guidance about the organization's priorities, ideals, and code of behavior. Organizations need very few key values that are personal to that organization which serve as anchors or guidelines just as honor, courage, and commitment do for the U.S. Marines.

4. **Communicate to the entire organization.** Communication is a process used to achieve understanding, agreement, and alignment, which are the goals of communication; creating communications is not the goal. When creating communications has become the goal, and that is very common in large organizations, the communication process is ineffective because people are bombarded by too many communications. The result is that there isn't enough focus and little stands out as really important. The number of communications in any period of time needs to be limited, although key messages need to be repeated many times. Especially when change is increasing people's level of anxiety and fear, messages need to be simple, focused, and repetitive. Communication about organizational change, for example, might be limited to answering three questions:

(a) Why do we have to change?

(b) What's involved?

(c) What positive and negative outcomes can be expected?

Large organizations need to focus on creating effective communication, especially with middle management and supervisors. Supervisors and mid-

dle managers have a lot of influence on the acceptance or rejection of proposed changes because most
employees really respect and "hear" the opinions of
their boss. That's why middle management and
supervisors play a critical role in terms of the success or failure of a change effort.

5. **Create aligned goals of the organization, units, and
   individuals.** A line of sight needs to be created
   between the organization's overarching goals and
   unit and individual performance targets. An organization's megagoals, for example, for the next year
   might be to:

   (a) increase profitability by 20 percent,
   (b) increase the retention of customers and
       employees by 30 percent, and
   (c) increase collaboration across the organization.

   Every unit and individual needs to commit to
   these goals by declaring what they will do in their
   function and job to achieve these organizational targets, and they need to decide on the dates when the
   goals will be accomplished. Although different functions, departments, and businesses make different
   contributions, a line of sight aligns the entire organization so everyone pursues what's considered most
   important at this time. Performance appraisals

should also create pressure on units, teams, and individuals so everyone is focused on achieving the organization's key objectives. Limiting the focus and aligning the organization's members speeds up the accomplishment of the organizationwide goals by several years.

6. **Decide whether people are thrivers, survivors, or strugglers.** This may well be the most important part of this change process. People can be divided into three groups in terms of whether or not they align with the goal of core change and the organization's new values. In IBM's terms, the three categories are thrivers, survivors, and strugglers (or failures).

Thrivers are people who usually have been outspoken in their criticism of the status quo. They've been calling for change, asserting that it's overdue. They're already aligned with the goal of change and want to be involved and make it happen. Because they're usually "wild ducks"—IBM's term for nonconformists—in stable times they're often regarded as nuisances. But in borderless conditions, they're natural allies of the change leaders. They can be anywhere in the organization, but a higher percentage are relatively new to the organization and often close to entry level. In addition to their view that major change is long overdue, thrivers tend to be models of the values, attitudes, and behaviors that have been newly designated as most desirable. Thrivers, therefore, are natural models for the rest of the organization. Change always requires significant carrots and sticks. Whether or not thrivers get a formal promotion, everyone in the organization needs to see them as winners. That's the carrot. Thrivers are winners and are clearly rewarded when they replace survivors and strugglers in decision-making roles. That's the stick. Thrivers are also first in line for education, training, and developmental experiences. Thrivers are rewarded visibly and significantly.

Thrivers must also be effective performers in terms of achieving goals in order to be role models. But it's more important that they have the right attitudes, values, and behaviors than the right skills, knowledge, and experience. Skills, knowledge, and experience are much easier to acquire than it is to change and gain the right attitudes, values, and behaviors. Mostly, thrivers act like the organization talks. Thrivers are a critical organizational resource and management should give most of its time and thought to people in this group.

Survivors have seen too many change programs launched...and fail, only to be replaced by the next effort. They've been disappointed too many times to remain optimistic or enthusiastic. Survivors stay on the sideline, neither joining in nor opposing, until they see whether or not real change is going to occur. Waiting and watching, at best, survivors are fence-sitters; at worst, they're cynics.

Many survivors, especially fence-sitters, will join the thrivers when they see it's both required and advantageous to do so. They will get on board when they see that real change is happening and thrivers are replacing some previous management people. It's a lot more fun to be treated as an organizational asset and a member of the club than it is to be seen as a liability.

Strugglers (or failures) are people who don't get it, and many never will. They fall into two groups: those who *can't* get it and those who *won't*. People who can't get on board, who can't manage job-related or personal changes, are people who never developed self-confidence. After a lifetime of avoiding risk and anything new, it's too late for them to develop the personal qualities that will allow them to be comfortable with basic change. Without confidence, any change is just too scary. Organizations need to make a decision about what they'll do with the *can't* struggler. In my experience, although their future is very limited, as long as they don't take a lot of management time, they're good workers, and the work they do continues to be necessary, they can be retained.

Won't strugglers are confident enough to be comfortable with even major change but they refuse to get on board. Instead, they actively try to impede the targeted changes. *Won'ts* are actively opposed to the change program and often display contempt for the program and its leaders. Most of them are bitter, believing they've been cheated out of something that was rightfully theirs, like a promotion or a corner office. "Getting their own," or revenge is usually part of their agenda. In my observations, they're very dangerous because they're centers of infection that can poison the views and attitudes of others. Their opposition is frequently hidden to management because they spread their negativism behind people's backs. Equally dangerous, they are not impacted by the "antibiotics" of peer pressure or rewards and punishments. That's why they need to be cut out.

7. **Fire troublemaking strugglers.** Evaluate the strugglers, especially the *won'ts*, in terms of how disruptive they are. Identify those who create the most problems and are most disliked. Select one or two from each unit. Tell the selected *won'ts* that their jobs are in danger because of their disruptive attitudes and obstructive behavior. Check with legal counsel for guidelines for firing them. Keep detailed records of all conversations and subsequent outcomes. Provide whatever coaching, counseling, training, or education that Legal and Human Resources suggest. If there is no significant improvement by the date Legal sets, fire them.

8. **Fire chronic nonperformers.** Because a key goal of a stable organization's change effort is to become performance driven, it's necessary to separate chronic nonperformers. Select several nonperform-

ers in each unit who obviously don't work and whom others resent because they have to do the work of the nonperformer. Provide whatever interventions Human Resources and Legal suggest, and keep excellent records of meetings, discussions, and actions. If there's insufficient improvement within the recommended amount of time, fire them.

For legal and psychological reasons it is important to give the *won'ts* and the nonperformers a fair chance to improve. First, a few of them might. Second, the message of fairness is very important to the rest of the organization. In the midst of borderless turbulence, people need the reassurance that decisions to terminate are not being made arbitrarily and without any chance of redemption. Firing uncooperative and nonproductive people after a fair process is an important signal to the rest of the survivors and strugglers. It communicates, "You'd better get on board while you still have time!" Some survivors, especially, will step off the platform and into the train.

9. **Start the process again.** Reassess the business goals and the people issues. Identify successes and decide if a previous organizational goal has been achieved enough for it to be replaced by a new one. Revisit impediments to success and identify continued or new problems. Prioritize issues and continue to pursue old goals or set new ones. Set target dates.

When the need for fundamental change is obvious, basic change can be accomplished over time if the leadership has determination and courage. Fear and panic about change give way to optimism and hope when the change program succeeds and the organization clearly does better as a result. Plan carefully because the change initiative must not fail. Failure is exhausting and demoralizing in the present and jeopardizes necessary changes in the future. Manage to success; people naturally flourish and want to participate where there's success.

15 INDIVIDUALS: CREATE A PROFOUNDLY SATISFYING LIFE

- SATISFY BOTH THE ME AND THE US IN YOUR LIFE
- KING MIDAS IS A BAD ROLE MODEL
- LIVE LIFE VIVIDLY—WITH A SENSE OF ADVENTURE

A cab driver, a curious and friendly man, initiated a remarkably open and searching conversation with me once. "I'm from Somalia," he said, "one of the poorest countries in the world. Sometimes people don't have anything to eat for tomorrow but yet, they are happy. And here, where you have so much, people are unhappy. Can you explain that?"

"Well," I replied, "I think that when you have very little, you don't expect much and you're very grateful for what you have. When hard work doesn't get you far, then you may not try very hard because the chances are good that it won't do much for you. So you try to look on the bright side of things."

"Two things are probably very important in terms of the difference between the United States and Somalia," I continued. "For one thing, we don't have an identity or status because we're someone's child or a member of a tribe. Our status and identity come from what we achieve. And unlike Somalia, hard work usually results in something good happening to you. So Americans usually work hard. The American Dream is to achieve a better life for yourself and especially for your children. While working very hard might look like unhappiness to outsiders, truth is, most Americans really love to work. In fact, many of us lead lopsided lives in which most of our energy goes into work. That certainly includes me."

When your life is unbalanced because you're deeply immersed in something you feel passionate about, you often get productive and creative. Great accomplishments, I think, usually require a laser-like focus. That's how I work. But unbalanced lives have an inherent danger: Although success is achieved in one sector of your life—usually your work or your family—when that sector is no longer exciting or fulfilling, there's nothing else in your life that's important enough to give you a powerful sense of being alive, or of being connected, or of being a good person.

That's why my life is a series of pendulum swings, arcing between the work-dominated unbalanced life that's natural to me and deliberate efforts to get some better balance. It was much easier to have a balanced life of work, family, community, and friends when my kids were young and their needs had to be met. It was as profoundly satisfying to see them develop and thrive as it was to achieve a professional breakthrough. But the empty nest that follows when children become adults, and the dispersion of the family across a wide geography, makes it pretty easy for people to pursue their own interests, the "me" in their lives. It doesn't take long for life to become unbalanced.

Although the workaholic life can be exhilarating, in the long run, life is profoundly satisfying and psychologically healthier when there's some balance between gratifying the needs of both "me" and "us." Without a commitment to some form of "us," to community or family or cause, many people's lives become shallow and therefore unfulfilling because they skirt along the surface of relationships and experiences. Most people need to engage in some human commitment that is greater than the self in order to feel their life is rich in relationships and experiences that matter.

The risk of burnout is very high when life is very narrowly focused on work. Americans know that: They are convinced that being a member of a strong family is essential to their sense of well-being. Survey after survey reports that although the vast majority of Americans are satisfied with their jobs, more than 90 percent say that achieving a better balance between work and home is a critical priority.

It's actually pretty simple: Human beings need emotional connections. People need friends and family and colleagues and neighbors and community. The workaholic lifestyle, in which the only commitment of passion is work, is intrinsically lonely because it's fundamentally narcissistic.

The workaholic lifestyle became more widespread in the borderless economy, especially in the second half of the 1990s. The unrelenting demands for better!, faster!, and cheaper!, in combination with the possibility of previously unimagined wealth, fueled widespread acceptance of a 24/7, heroic work-dominated life. The result is that many people felt or feel less connected within their families, while, at the same time, they became more dependent on it for emotional support. It also became easier to feel unconnected, unsupported, or isolated because many communities are new and so are the people who have moved into them.

We live in a very small 10-year-old development in Southern California. The only people who seem to have relationships with their neighbors are the people who walk their dogs several times a day. Many years ago we lived in a neighborhood that was full of friendships because everyone had young kids, and the kids all played together. We had a strong sense of community because the grammar school, kindergarten through the eighth grade, was two blocks away in the center of the neighborhood. The neighborhood we live in now is too expensive for young people so we have virtually no kids and certainly no school, stores, churches, or parks. So, even though this development is composed of only four streets, there isn't a community of people.

A workaholic lifestyle, a fragile nuclear family, geographic separation from the extended family, the absence of roots in the community, and widespread feelings of isolation are challenging issues for the United States.

Nothing much ever happens on a big scale until it's almost too late. It's now almost too late and, thus, it's time to become optimistic. As stress levels soar, people create new anchors of stability. When the external world feels out of control, people architect new ways to connect and regain control. People will increase the importance of their internal world where they have greater control, and that is largely a focus on their world of family.

It is no accident that America is in the midst of a baby boom. People are putting more energy and time into their nuclear family—even if it's the second or third time—and men as well as women are making the parenting role more and more important. Our kids have much more contact with each other and with us than they used to five, much less 10 years ago. Getting together has become a seriously high priority for all of us and that includes the extended family and those friends who are close enough to be thought of as family.

When stress is chronic and life feels both too busy and

yet unfulfilled, people create new ways to connect and regain control. People and their institutions try to achieve adaptations to the new reality, including new ways to meet our most human needs at work. Let the experiments begin!

Paul Eichen was always driven by the need to succeed. As CEO of Proxima Corp, he led the business' growth to over $100 million. It was about then that he realized that his life was work and it had cost him a great deal.[1] He then decided he would build a new company, one that was financially successful and that contributed to a life that was balanced and healthy. Every decision of the new company was to be based on the answer to the questions: How would this make work feel? How would this knit life and work together? He set out to create a company that would make life good.

Thus far, Eichen is succeeding. His company, the Rokenbok Toy Company, makes sophisticated toys like their Monorail set which uses cutting-edge technology to create one-of-a-kind radio-controlled vehicles and an interactive cityscape. In five years, Eichen's toy company established a brand, won accolades from the industry, and is on track to reach $12 million in revenues. Located near the beach in Encinitas, California, the policy on dress is casual, people's kids hang out at the company, and employees come and go on bicycles. As long as people do their work, they can set their own hours. There's intellectual stimulation and socializing and the excitement of competing and winning.

Rokenbok's employees are encouraged to think of them-selves as people who need to satisfy both the "me" and "us" in their lives. The company wants its people to achieve success in both life and work. The result, so far, is that Rokenbok's employees are fulfilled at work and they're happy with their lives.

Our commitments should not be narrowed to that of work or family, and indeed, they need not be narrowed to those of work and family. Life can involve commitments to institutions—domestic or international, political or social—or to people, strangers as well as friends, needy or just interesting. The important point is that life has to include more than just "me."

Although there still aren't many companies with Paul Eichen's very explicit commitment to fostering employees' personal lives hand-in-glove with achieving business success, there is a real range in terms of how humane or family-friendly organizations are. People who want to work full out, who want to expand their commitments to include more than work, or make their commitment to family equal to or greater than their commitment to work all need to determine what the real policies of organizations are, as they must also learn the outcomes of working alone. Then, they need to choose what they will do because we are each responsible for creating our personal best fit, with the goal of creating lives that are deeply satisfying and fulfilling.

Although the 1990s economy flourished, it came at a

cost to many of those who worked in it. It is both good business and humane to acknowledge that, in the long run, we have to deal with the human issues in order to achieve lasting organizational success as well as individual fulfillment. The Rokenbok Toy Company is part of a small stream of life and work experiments that are likely to expand when the economy recovers. It's possible that the stream could become a broad river because the stock market decline, the death of dot-coms, and the downturn in the economy led many workaholics to conclude that the cost of a life dedicated only to work, can be the loss of a fulfilling life.

KING MIDAS AND THE NEED FOR IDEALISM

> You'd better not end up like Granddad, Dad, [Nicola said to her father Andy on more than one occasion.] 'Cause I plan to spend all my money on me.
>
> Yet it really wasn't avarice that dominated her behavior. Rather, it seemed to be a profound vacuity at the heart of her that she sought to fill with material possessions...And when she acquired what she had begged to possess, she wasn't able to see that it satisfied her only briefly. Her vision was occluded from this knowledge because what stood in the way was always the desire for the next object that she believed would soothe her soul.[2]

In the last decade of the 20th century, the American economy created a period of the greatest growth and prosperity ever seen.[3] Is it a perfectly reasonable choice to elevate work to one's highest commitment and work 24/7 to earn $1 million or $5 million or $10 million? Given the choice, would the majority of Americans pursue a goal of a lifetime of financial security? Of course they would! Why, then, is a cautionary note in order?

In a tale as old as King Midas, a workaholic life in the pursuit of money for its own sake often turns out badly. When money is the only goal, the outcome is often psychological isolation, narcissism, and greed.

The pursuit of any single goal to the exclusion of anything else usually ends badly because when the goal is achieved, it's rarely satisfying for long. That's especially true for money. If money isn't a by-product of a goal that has some personal meaning, most people find the sheer accumulation of money or the things it can buy pretty empty after a while. So it makes perfect psychological sense that most of the time, the "me" goal of making money is combined with an "us" goal like building a company and creating jobs or giving a serious amount of the money that's made to institutions or causes that are important to the donor.[4]

Pursuing money for its own sake often makes people selfish. That's why people need to bond financial goals with ideals. The human spirit wants a life well lived and that requires goals and accomplishments that satisfy the soul. Wealth is a richer outcome when people can see that they also achieved something enduring, something beneficial, something good. Without the feeling your life made a difference, when it's close to over, many people challenge themselves: "Did it matter that I lived? What is my legacy?"

Life is fuller when goals include ideals. I remember when John F. Kennedy came to the University of Michigan and delivered his Peace Corps speech on the steps of the Michigan Union. We were thrilled by the spirit of his words: "Do not ask what your country can do for you, but ask what you can do for your country."[5] We were patriots then and we were thrilled. There was a profound appeal in the idea of adventure combined with noble service.

In the winter of 2000, Senator John McCain looked, for a while, like he might win his party's nomination to run for the presidency. McCain tapped into that same vein of patriotism and service that Kennedy had and many people were inspired. He called on his audience, especially the young people, to become engaged in our democracy and to serve in a cause: Join the military, teach, work in health care, or help the poor, he said, commit to something greater than yourself. Recommit, he called, to the idea of America and to the virtues of honor, courage, integrity, and duty, which are necessary and integral to keeping the nation great.

In the midst of an extraordinary economy, McCain appealed to crowds who yearned for something more than material success. The sociologist Marvin Bressler calls this "holiness," a sense that what one does has meaning and contributes to something greater than ourselves.[6]

The same kind of idealism can sometimes be found in

successful businesses. Although Charles Schwab started his discount brokerage in order to make money, he was also convinced that it would succeed if the company really served its customers by being the most useful and ethical brokerage in the country.[7] In their employee surveys, Schwab's people keep saying, "This job gives me a chance to serve others; a chance to make a difference; a chance to leave a personal legacy that is meaningful."

Kim Polese, cofounder and formerly CEO of Marimba Inc., a software company in Silicon Valley, is a passionate advocate of having values and ideals.[8] She believes that people stay in a company because that organization is changing the world in ways they admire and they want to be a part of that. What really matters to people, she says, is being part of the team, having a mission, and creating something. That, Polese says, "is what turns people on. That's what life is about."

At heart, our life is made up of choices we make that can be thought of as a surge and flow between the polarities of the narcissistic "me" and the communal "us."

It is in the very nature of humans that people have two very basic motives and they appear to be in conflict. People want to both maximize self-interest and gain something for themselves, and they also want to be idealistic and do something that contributes to the greater good. Idealism is often less obvious than self-interest, but it is very powerful. In short, people want the opportunity to achieve and be recognized and rewarded—and they also want to make a contribution that expands their soul and makes a difference. Wise people make sure their choices include both.

IT'S YOUR LIFE

For one year, from June 1973 through June 1974, my husband, our three kids, and I lived in a 21-foot Winnebago while we wandered through Central and South America. It was an extraordinary experience: We never knew what was down the road and around the corner. We didn't know who we'd meet, what we'd eat, or where we'd sleep. That was the thrill of it. Even if it was a bad day, it was a vivid day.

At that time it had become important for my husband and me to set out on a voyage of discovery. It was less an exploration of foreign cultures than it was a discovery of ourselves. We had come to the realization that in the career-dominated pattern of our lives, we had let the rest of our commitments plateau. We had allowed life and relationships to become habitual. Anything that becomes routine is not really experienced. It was only in work that we were passionately alive and so we had become workaholics. To recapture life we had to take work out of our lives.

The next time you walk through the door of your home, pay attention to how much you see. Your home is filled with things you selected. You chose the furniture, the rugs, and all of those decorative objects...many of which were probably bought on trips which makes them doubly special. But the reality is, when you walk through the door of your home you don't see anything because it has all become too familiar.

The opposite of vivid is routine, the enemy of a life that is rich in experience. Most people allow their lives to gradually fall into narrow and deep routines. We see the same close friends and have the same conversations week after week. We go out to dinner every Saturday. Friends and family come over for lunch on Sunday. Although routines are often comfortable, they are always deadening. A repetitious life is a life that is flat; it has plateaued.[9]

Everyone, but especially workaholics, need the equivalent of a Winnebago adventure, even if it's on a small scale. It's not hard to achieve. I've been doing hatha yoga first thing in the morning for over thirty years. It's also been our practice to hike the mountain we live on at the close of the workday. One day we hiked first thing in the morning: What a revelation that was! The light that permeates our landscape was different: It was luminescent. The streets were filled with people—which we never see—and they smiled and waved. It was a great beginning to the day. To get off a life plateau, just do some things differently: Create an adventure, face up to a new challenge, or find something that makes you gasp or smile or sing.

I recently saw a photograph of my mother when she was

a beautiful young woman of 21, with me, at about one year old. It's not possible to see that image and merge it with that of my mother seen through the lens of age. Life is so fleeting. Therefore, live life vividly and with some sense of adventure.

To have a worthwhile life, achieve some things you believe are important. As long as there are commitments or goals or issues you care about, then your work can be significant—to you. It is another issue, and not nearly as important, whether or not your work made a significant difference to the world. To put that in perspective, most people's work is interchangeable. It doesn't matter who did it. Doctors in clinics as well as shoe salesmen in malls are interchangeable. But parents are not. That's why a lot of people, perhaps the majority, find their most significant work in raising their children.

A soaring stock market, exuberant excess in consumer spending, and the millionaire neighbors next door, in combination with the borderless world's relentless demands to do it better!, faster!, and cheaper!, led many Americans in the 1990s toward a life dominated by the priorities of work. We not only gave work the largest amount of our time, we gave it the largest amount of our passion, and we paid too little attention to the fact that a work-absorbed life is also a commitment primarily to "me."

There is no lifestyle that is the best for everyone, but it is fair to say that no life is best satisfied by meeting the needs of "me" or "us." At different stages of life, "me" or "us" will loom larger or smaller, but in the longer term the narcissistic workaholic needs an "us" commitment in order to feel grounded and the "us"committed person needs to gratify "me" or resentment of those they are caring for follows.

September 11, 2001, woke Americans up to the fact that although work and success are often exciting and engrossing, it's the quality of your life that's always at stake and our lives require connecting as well as succeeding. Everyone needs to have an "us" and a "me" in their life. I wish everyone a life filled with experience and a legacy they're proud of, based on values and commitments that make life rich and meaningful. If we pay conscious attention to what really matters to us, make decisions that are a best fit, and use life's plateaus to revitalize ourselves, we all can and should achieve a life that satisfies and matters.

ENDNOTES

1. Hopkins, Michael, "The Pursuit of Happiness," *Inc.*, August 2000, pp. 72–90.

2. George, Elizabeth, *In Pursuit of the Proper Sinner*, Bantam Books, New York, November 2000, p. 645–646.

3. At a dinner party in the spring of 2000, everyone told stories about people they knew who had just fallen into serious wealth. My personal favorite was the tale of a couple who had just made $17 million by cashing in their options from companies they'd been pushed out of.

4. No, I haven't forgotten the tax advantages. The point is that there are psychological as well as financial gains when ideals are married to behavior.

5. Kennedy, John Fitzgerald, Remarks proposing a Peace Corps, October 14, 1960; Quote from the inaugural address, January 20, 1961.

6. Bressler, Marvin, in *The HR Imperative*, The Concours Group, September 1988.

7. Pottruck, David S., and Pearce, Terry, "Creating Culture," *Business 2.0*, May 2000, pp. 362–378.

8. Petzinger Thomas, Jr., "Talking About Tomorrow: Kim Polese," *The Wall Street Journal*, January 1, 2000, p. R24.

9. For more information about plateauing, see my book, *The Plateauing Trap*, AMACOM, New York, 1991.

Appendix

The following questionnaires are presented to facilitate a best fit between employees and organizations:

Questionnaire I: This Organization Is:

Questionnaire II: I Want:

TABLE A-1 This Organization Is:
(Score 1 to 3) 1 = not very, 2 = pretty much, 3 = very much so

CHARACTERISTIC	SCORE	
	Today	In 2 years
Calm and deliberate		
Fast and decisive		
Very high risk		
Low to medium risk		
Entrepreneurial		
Slow. People wait for orders. Polite		
Characterized by forthright challenges		
Filled with an intense hum		
Filled with people who think like employees		
Dominated by seniority		
One where only results count		
Filled with high risk/high return excitement		
Quiet, comfortable and there are few surprises		
Focused on business outcomes		
Dominated by staff and professionals		
Internally competitive		
Characterized by collegial relationships		
One in which results outweigh status		
One in which status outweighs results		
One in which people tolerate boring work		
Learning and challenge are ongoing		
Exceeding personal expectations is vital		
Achieving success is immensely important		
One in which people don't play together		
One where having fun with colleagues is valued		
One where individualism is a core value		
One where people expect everyone to be treated the same regardless of contribution		

TABLE A-2 | want:

(Score 1 to 3) 1 = not very, 2 = pretty much, 3 = very much so

CHARACTERISTIC	SCORE	
My work assignments customized		
More flexible work arrangements		
Reasonable work hours		
Choice about benefits		
Choice about forms of compensation		
Opportunities to work on my ideas		
Options and a chance to get rich		
More autonomy		
Opportunities to make decisions and lead		
Work to be an exciting place		
Very clear goals and deadlines		
Training/education		
Predictability and some job security		
The latest tools		
To work with the smartest people		
Fun colleagues		
To do important, cutting-edge work		
Opportunities to initiate		
Freedom to innovate		

AFTERWORD

J. Peter Bardwick

S *ome people like the roller coaster, some people like the merry-go-round. Successful executives in today's business world probably need to be roller coaster fans.*

It's an interesting time to be in the business world. Nothing motivates introspection like making a public fool of oneself. And in the short time from the dot-com boom to bust, many executives have gone from having all the answers to having none. My slightly bloody experience tells me that technology has truly changed the art of management, and there are no successful businesses without artful management. Clearly, many attributes important to successful management are constant: No organization can achieve long-term success without leadership, shared vision, effective communications, honesty, skillful execution, and a powerful work ethic. But pervasive technology has had a fundamental impact on the skills needed to manage businesses.

Early in my career, management skills didn't seem particularly pertinent. Now that I am older and wiser, that seems a pretty astounding statement. Business schools preach that Human Resources is important, but it's not something an interviewer is likely to ask about. After business school, I went to Wall Street, where senior management is an oxymoron. Succeeding on Wall Street takes myriad talents—smarts, sales skills, competitiveness, political savvy, and a nose for money. But none of this prepares one to actually manage people. I worked on Wall Street in the heyday of leveraged buyouts and junk bonds when there was too much money to be made to "waste time" on managing. And when the heyday ended management's task was simply to cut the head count.

My move from Wall Street to the corporate world came when I was asked by a client to become vice president of finance and help them through a severe financial crisis. I did, thus making the transition into management. The more I encountered (and became responsible for) successful and unsuccessful companies in the borderless world, the more I became intrigued with management. This is a venture capital truism: A great management team with an OK product will always beat an OK management team with a great product. We clearly see this in the aftermath of the dot-com bubble. The companies that have survived and will eventually thrive are invariably led by great teams. Managing a company well is probably the most fascinating, difficult, and underrated job around—it's a 3-D chess game and the timer never stops. Recent experiences building companies in the dot-com world convince me that management has gotten harder and become even more important: Pervasive technology has accelerated the pace of change for every aspect of business.

So where is the roller coaster? It starts the minute you enter any borderless organization. In borderless companies you can't find the merry-go-round. It's in the archives with the sepia picture of the founders, the Selectric typewriter, and the ticker tape.

PRESS THE FLESH

Surprisingly, in technology-driven borderless companies, personal touch has become more critical than ever. One of the least appreciated effects of pervasive technology is the need to nurture personal relationships, inside and outside the organization. The stereotype of a borderless company is globally distributed workers, suppliers, and customers, all communicating smoothlessly. The same technology that enables this communication creates distance between people: Business gets done between people you know and trust.

As a manager, I've sent corporatewide weekly email updates and felt that I've communicated well. Too often I've expressed what I thought was important, but have not addressed people's real concerns. Electronic communication doesn't allow for nuance, reaction, body language, or intuition. This is as true for customers and suppliers as it is for employees. With busy schedules, the "efficiency" of sending a string of emails feels good and can lull us into thinking that we are progressing. It's depressingly common to enter a meeting thinking that issues have been resolved only to find that people hold different assumptions and agreement is still far off.

One of the major claims of the Internet is that it makes communications easier. Data comes through email, corporate intranets, Internet sites, and online media. Counterintuitively, the prevalence of electronic communications makes management's task harder and effective communication skills more important. Like a TV show with too many commercials, a blizzard of electronic information gets tuned out. The irony of ubiquitous electronic communication is that it can create a false sense of productive interaction. E-communication also makes it easy to hide behind the medium and avoid the sometimes difficult interactions that create good decisions and candid relationships. For managers who are uncomfortable dealing with the human side of business, e-communications can become a "silicon curtain."

You Can Run, but You Can't Hide

That corporations rely heavily on information technology isn't new. What's new is its ubiquity across the workplace: The PC on the CEO's desk is connected to every employee in the company, and every CEO around the globe. The common theme of transforming technologies is clearly the accelerating speed with which information is available, its sheer quantity, and its broad distribution.

Essentially, every desk in corporate America has a computer. Five years ago you might have heard an executive boast that he or she didn't use a PC or email. Today such an admission would be incomprehensible because technology represents both a significant expense and a source of competitive strength. A transforming change has been the dispersion of technology decision making. Traditionally these decisions have been handled by CEOs, CFOs, and CIOs. But with technology now at every level, heads of traditionally "soft" areas such as Human Resources, Sales, and Marketing have significant IT responsibilities. Successful borderless companies foster technical education and knowledge regardless of job description. Conversely, it is incumbent upon those traditionally responsible for IT to gain a more thorough understanding of the soft aspects of the business. IT managers are increasingly responsible for installing and maintaining systems that support these areas and they can't build good systems without understanding the problems being solved.

FORESTS AND TREES

With the wiring of the corporation, its suppliers, and customers, management is required to make real-time decisions in an environment of accelerating speed and complexity. Unfortunately, designing technology to produce relevant information that is easily understood and acted upon has proven to be very difficult. Even the most technologically savvy companies fail to understand and act upon their data. In May 2001, Cisco Systems (one of the world's most wired companies) took a $2.25 billion charge to write down inventory. Although Cisco surely has excellent data on its order pipeline and supply chain, the company was unable to use its data to respond effectively to industry conditions. Where management used to wait for market studies, cost analyses, and competitor's reactions, today's decisions often need to be made in real time with difficult-to-evaluate data. Thus, the availability of almost unlimited real-time data makes the "old-fashioned" skill of seat-of-the-pants decision making more important than ever.

NEED FOR SPEED

In a borderless economy, speed and certainty in decision making become paramount. This doesn't mean the dot-com fallacy that first movers always win. Rather, a management team will be more effective making 10 decisions in a week with three wrong than one making the same decisions over a month, with only one wrong. Few decisions are company killers and good organizations constantly make midcourse corrections. Fluid forward movement creates a Darwinian perfecting of the business model.

Communication of clear corporate goals, strategies, and tactics has never been more important because in border-less organizations time is short and decision making is broadly distributed. Rapid decision making must be supported by a common understanding of the organization's aims. This understanding creates the framework for effective collective action. One of the most common causes of failure among dot-coms was a lack of well-articulated and commonly understood goals. Companies grew so rapidly that new employees never gained that understanding. Commonly, management teams were too busy fighting fires (or hiding behind the silicon curtain) to create effective and consistent communications.

CONFIDENCE AND INTUITION

Rapid and effective decision-making requires confidence and intuition. Confidence is learned by making mistakes and working through them in a self-reinforcing process. The more you do it, the better it works. Borderless organizations have to build a tolerance for failure and an environment that encourages venturesome employees. In my experience, good intuition is really confidence in conjunction with a superior knowledge of the business. It's synthesizing all those pieces on the 3-D chessboard and acting on it. Creating effective employees is really about nurturing confidence and a broad knowledge of the company and its industry. Interestingly, this argues against the frequent job-hopping seen in young technology companies. It takes time to build intuition.

MANAGING THE UNMANAGEABLE

In borderless companies, many employees have job requirements and access to information that is not dissimilar to that of senior executives. These employees have smaller spans of control but are required to assimilate and act upon data with the same speed and certainty as the organization's CEO. Centralized management is simply incapable of handling the amount of information hitting the desktop daily. The wiring of the corporation has brought the information necessary for decision making to every level and created the tools to act upon that information. Today's employees are knowledgeable and empowered in a way that was incomprehensible 10 years ago. Employees who are effective in this role will always choose the roller coaster. Recruiting and managing this group requires the same skills as recruiting and managing a good CEO. They need autonomy, challenges, opportunities to learn, support for failures, and concrete—if difficult—goals. And in a traditional sense, they may not be manageable. The best environment for these employees is one with clear goals but significant leeway in how to achieve those goals. These employees will either control their destinies or find a place where they can.

Successful borderless companies are about enjoying risk, uncertainty, management of difficult-to-manage employees, and information overload. They are also about some very traditional traits like looking stakeholders in the eye and speaking the truth. The absense of certainty in this environment makes it all about enjoying the ride—the roller coaster—because you may not be able to control the destination.

AFTERWORD

Stephen R. Hardis

At a time when business managers are all into (or should be) root cause analysis, one starting point in gaining an understanding of the management challenge in today's technology-driven work environment is to reflect upon the overuse of the term revolution. Hyperbole has proven to be a contagious condition in every form of communication. We don't get weather reports; we get warnings. A 1 percent stock market movement is a major rally, and, in that same way, no one talks about trends, evolution, or changes in business. We note (with appropriate swelling background music) revolutions in technology, communications, competition, international trade, and every other noteworthy development.

Revolutions have become the rallying cries for radical new organizational modalities. Why worry about interpersonal relationships when we operate in a virtual state? Why worry about workplace tension when we are on a shared quest to get rich quick? Every business problem's solution is presumed to be the next software generation (Mod X is the ultimate panacea).

That would all be fine if business, as a result of techno-logical transformation, was truly mechanistic. The compli-cating factors, time and again, arise from the unavoidable truth that business still is (and always will be) a function of people. People have some enduring, unavoidable qualities: They mistrust change unless it is demonstrably in their self-interest, they mistrust management because of two decades of what they see as broken promises, and they mistrust hav-ing stock price as the ultimate goal because it too often appears ephemeral and capricious.

The dirty secret is that no technological breakthrough is going to be the basis for a successful, ongoing enterprise—unless one's goal is only to make it through an IPO and lock-up period—unless you solve the people problems: those minor issues such as motivation, leadership, communica-tions, trust, recruitment and retention, training and devel-opment, and, if you will, inspiration.

But these problems have to be solved in a markedly new environment. Electronic communications has become a critical tool, but it is intrusive, depersonalizing, and smoth-ering. Information (or, if you will, digital) technology has become the indispensable enabling tool, but it's usually unclear who is actually the master and whether there is going to be an ultimate win. Like two scorpions in the bot-tom of a bottle, we are constantly involved in a curious mat-ing dance with our new technological wonders, afraid to dis-engage, but also worried about our own survival.

In my view, what we are all struggling to do is to define

a new social contract with our people, one that embodies the proven elements of the past, with the new requisites of the present. It has to have more substance than is offered by the existentialist world of the stock market. We have broken faith so often that we can't appeal to traditional loyalties, but instead, we have to gain a better understanding of the mutual benefit gained and offered through enduring relationships. Individuals have to be compensated generously for the value they create; at the same time, no organization has staying power if it is peopled exclusively by mercenaries.

The cult of performance metrics, measured in real time with an instant perspective, drives managers to drive their people without an adequate consideration of their human needs. Business schools not only must begin to teach business ethics; they have to teach future executives how and when to compromise short-term performance to gain long-term enthusiasm. We do preventative maintenance on equipment, and our people are entitled to at least as much forethought.

A social contract implies mutual benefit, obligations, and understanding. It should be more than an asterisk in an offering memorandum. Instead, it should be the distillate of what we have learned about what it takes to optimize the symbiotic relationship between the company and the individual. Even in the crush to get in and then out of the world of dot-coms, there is time to recognize the need for an equivalent of a corporate golden rule.

This brings us back to the question of whether we live in revolutionary times. I would argue not. Ever since the start of the industrial revolution, we have been involved in dialectic. New technologies offer the promise of enhanced productivity at the cost of destabilizing the status quo. This forces a process of adjustment and alignment. Out of this process develops the capability to exploit the new technology, but also to create a fertile basis to encourage the invention of newer technologies. By historic standards, today's technological wonders are not relatively more significant than a whole series of major innovations that emerged over the past two centuries. Much of what so impresses us now has its roots in intellectual breakthroughs from the 1920s.

Our conceit has been to overlook history and claim that we are living in unprecedented times. Thus, we coin "new economy" to distinguish what interests us now, from what existed before. Impatient for instant gratification, we joyously join the mob in the latest new stock market fad. Market bubbles emerge, grow, and explode long before we demand rational business plans. Older, experienced managers are bypassed because "they don't get it" in the rush to harness the energy and creativity of the young. The biological tropism toward young bodies is well proven, but this is the first time we have entrusted the stewardship of major businesses on the basis of these urges.

This may sound like angry words from someone eligible for a senior discount on movie tickets. But it also represents over forty years of business experience. In that time, I learned that there is no substitute for one-on-one human contact, in which you really listen to the other person, rather than treating it as another opportunity "to spread the word." Loyalty can only be built on a foundation of trust, and trust is always a function of candor and honesty. Drawing organization charts is fun for some people; I prefer trying to figure out how to position individuals so that they have the best chance of succeeding. Above all, experience has proven to me that the individuals on the line, closest to the action, know the most about the business and what is required to meet customers' expectations. My job was to motivate, not to direct.

It's time we recognize the need to pace our ambitions to the needs of our people. Let's be sure that we are bringing them solutions, not endless new challenges. A starting point would be to define performance in traditional human terms, not simply by the stock price. When we ritualistically intone that our people are our most important asset, let's at least pause long enough to ponder the implications of that mantra before we initiate yet another restructuring program…and, yes, let's allow our people to lead.

INDEX